Evolutionary Financial Macroeconomics

T0358886

Thorstein Veblen and Hyman Minsky are seminal thinkers who place great importance on the interaction between processes that link finance and financial markets with economic and social evolution. This book makes a contribution to the recontextualisation of the habitual, non-evolutionary and laissez-faire macroeconomic theory and policy, thus exposing the relevant contribution of the macro-theories of Veblen and Minsky.

The book starts with an elucidation of Veblen's cultural theory of insufficient private demand, waste and financial fragility and instability. It shows how speculative and parasitic leverage engenders solvency illusions and risk, pecuniary efficiency, low quality liability structures and socially destructive boom-bust cycles. Minsky's creative destruction liquidity processes and coordination failures of cash flow escalate the aforementioned path-dependent developments and explosive dynamics of capitalist economies. The main themes of the book are the cultural, evolutionary and holistic vision of macroeconomics, the evolving habits of mind, routines and financial institutions, the speculative, manipulated and unstable financial markets, as well as the financial macroeconomic destabilizing effects of pecuniary and parasitic consumption and investment.

This book will be of great interest to researchers, intellectuals and students pursuing economics and finance.

Giorgos Argitis, Professor of Macroeconomics, Department of Economics, National and Kapodistrian University of Athens, Greece.

Routledge Critical Studies in Finance and Stability

Edited by Jan Toporowski, *School of Oriental and African Studies, University of London, UK*

The 2007–8 Banking Crash has induced a major and wide-ranging discussion on the subject of financial (in)stability and a need to revaluate theory and policy. The response of policy-makers to the crisis has been to refocus fiscal and monetary policy on financial stabilisation and reconstruction. However, this has been done with only vague ideas of bank recapitalisation and 'Keynesian' reflation aroused by the exigencies of the crisis, rather than the application of any systematic theory or theories of financial instability.

Routledge Critical Studies in Finance and Stability covers a range of issues in the area of finance including instability, systemic failure, financial macroeconomics in the vein of Hyman P. Minsky, Ben Bernanke and Mark Gertler, central bank operations, financial regulation, developing countries and financial crises, new portfolio theory and New International Monetary and Financial Architecture.

For more information about this series, please visit www.routledge.com/series/RCSFS

Evolutionary Financial Macroeconomics

Giorgos Argitis

Routledge
Taylor & Francis Group

LONDON AND NEW YORK

First published 2020 by Routledge

2 Park Square, Milton Park, Abingdon, Oxon, OX14 4RN
605 Third Avenue, New York, NY 10017

Routledge is an imprint of the Taylor & Francis Group, an informa business

First issued in paperback 2020

British Library Cataloguing in Publication Data
A catalogue record for this book is available from the British Library

Library of Congress Cataloging-in-Publication Data
A catalog record has been requested for this book

ISBN: 978-1-138-05996-2 (hbk)
ISBN: 978-0-367-77731-9 (pbk)

Typeset in Bembo
by Taylor & Francis Books

To Stella, Anna and Vasilis

Contents

Preface

This book has been written in response to current debates that have brought forward the need for a reassessment of the current state of macroeconomic theory and policy. This need is even more imperative in the post global financial crisis period, which has evidenced the profound failure of habitual, equilibrium and laissez-faire macroeconomics to provide a pragmatic comprehension of the financial processes that generate frequent episodes of insolvent and unsustainable balance sheets, asset price bubbles and credit crunches, fragility and instability, debt-deflation, business cycles and stagnation tendencies.

The writer's key objective is to expose the enduring value and relevance of the macro-visions of Veblen and Minsky so as the readers can comprehend better the explosive dynamics and intrinsic instability of an accumulating capitalist economy with complex, evolving and unstable financial markets. The central argument of this book is that Veblen and Minsky placed solvency, liquidity and the endogenous fragility of the financial system at the heart of their evolutionary understanding of macroeconomics. The writer is of the opinion that a mixture of Veblen's post-Darwinian cultural macroeconomic theory with Minsky's Schumpeterian evolutionary macro-finance approach to capitalist instability adds value to the building of foundations necessary for the development of a cultural, holistic, evolutionary macroeconomic theory.

The value added contains a pragmatic bias in the understanding of the interconnection between financial fragility and macroeconomic change. It also encompasses likely guidelines for institutional reforms and macroeconomic policy interventions to reinforce coherence and promote employment, security and welfare. Particular attention is focused on the cultural foundations of the principle of effective demand and of how speculative and parasitic credit creation, unsustainable leverage and liability structures and solvency illusions engender industrial inefficiency, waste, unemployment, inequality and socially destructive boom-bust cycles.

Giorgos Argitis

Introduction

In the last decades, the global economy finds itself entrapped in an apparently boundless process of corporate scandals, frauds, asset prices bubbles, severe stock market fluctuations and credit booms and crashes. Above and beyond, in 2007–2008, the global economy experienced the destructive consequences of the speculative collapse of an enormous debt-financed housing bubble. All these episodes have delivered fresh evidence that modern accumulating capitalist economies, which are distinguished by complex and evolving financial institutions and structures, are inherently unstable and their growth and welfare dynamics are unsustainable. Besides, these episodes have brought to the fore the risks, dangers and effects of the increasing financialisation of contemporary capitalism.

The 'Great Crash' has also uncovered that speculative and fraudulent activities, fragile and low-quality household, corporate and banking balance sheets, bankruptcies, financial innovation and profit-seeking competition and risk-taking management interrelate with income inequality, insecurity, unemployment and insufficient demand. In combination they launch a crisis of performance and public confidence. The crisis of confidence, in turn, put in doubt the ethics and the culture of financial institutions and business corporations and, ultimately, the viability of capitalist economies.

Furthermore, the outburst of the 'Great Crash' and its aftermath called into question the economic orthodoxy in both scientific and philosophical levels. Looking at the conceptual structure of habitual macroeconomics one can easily detect its failure to escape from customary and unrealistic preconceptions concerning the structure and functioning of real-world economies. The anti-pragmatic bias and the analytical routines of the neoclassical theory (in all its forms) surmise the value of universally valid assumptions and axioms free from history and institutions that, eventually, construct a highly abstract system of general relations. The end result is that this theoretical system habitualises the economic profession and policy-makers to a market-clearing, self-equilibrating and acultural homo economicus world.

However, the creation and the burst of the recent debt-financed bubble validate that finance and financial markets have become powerful, influential and, mostly, fragile and unstable. In addition, they uncover that crashes and recessions in real-world economies can be brought about by a private sector that prefers to maximise its indebtedness, rather than maximising profits and full-employment output. Besides, an over-leveraged private sector is very possible to create a need for the minimisation of its debt-dependence, if it becomes apparent that the liabilities created are unsustainable. However, this fact is unreasonably demoted by conventional macroeconomics. It is very logical that economic units, which are unable to fulfil debt commitments, prefer to pay down their inherited debt and cut down their consumption and investment spending so as to restore their solvency and creditworthiness. Therefore, in debt-driven production economies, financial macroeconomic instability, debt-deflation and recession are conceivable. The economic and financial history of capitalism has evidenced that the evolution of the financial system brings significant structural and organisational changes and shifts in behavioural patterns. These effects have become even more commanding as debt grows rapidly, often even more rapidly than nominal gross national product. In this vein, habitual macroeconomics cannot be the basis for fruitful research on the behaviour of modern market economies and for drawing useful economic policies to stabilise them. Macroeconomic theory and policy must come opposite to the real facts of economic experience.

The principal thesis of this book is that a comprehensive understanding of the rapid change and instability of modern capitalist economies would seek macro-economic theory to be preferably away from equilibrium, acultural and non-monetary conceptual frameworks. Let it be known that within these frameworks there are no speculation, no manipulation, no unsustainable and insolvent balance sheets, no coordination failures between cash inflows and cash outflows, no bubbles and no crashes. Moreover, macroeconomic theory should also distance itself from laissez-faire policy illusions. If financial fragility, instability and crisis are fundamental features of economic processes that go forward in calendar time, then speculation, securitisation, rising debt-service ratio, liquidation, insolvency, deleverage and bankruptcies would all appear as common facts and fully endogenous proprieties of capitalist economies, which evolve under the destabilising impact of pecuniary habits of thought, manipulation, fraudulent activities and financial innovation and competition. The rapid financialisation of modern economies has thoroughly increased the debt-financed spending by households, business firms, and governments rising complexity and uncertainty. To understand the structure, performance and fragility of modern market economies that have become profoundly weighted by layered private and public debts, we need a financial macro-vision that embraces institutional links between the quality and sustainability of leverage and liability structures and changes in income distribution, effective demand and waste.

In order to do so, macroeconomics needs a conceptual recontextualisation of the habitual theorisation of macroeconomic affairs. Macroeconomics needs a new vision that would institutionalise new preconceptions and habits of mind about the world of reality. This book stresses that such a reconception and recontextualisation should noticeably incorporate a cultural, holistic, financial dynamic theorising of the realities of modern capitalism. In this respect, this book delves into the writings of Thorstein Veblen and of Hyman Minsky, in order to disclose the enduring value of their financial and macroeconomic ideas and their importance for enlarging the building of foundations for an evolutionary understanding of macroeconomics. With that in mind, I organise the book around some of central concepts of Veblen's and Minsky's macro-visions, which establish three foundational principles for the comprehension of change in real-world macro-systems: evolving financial institutions, unsustainable leverage and liability structures and insufficient demand. These foundational principles blend Veblen's post-Darwinian cultural macroeconomics with Minsky's Schumpeterian financial macroeconomics. In my opinion, this mixture adds value to the contextualisation of an evolutionary theory of macroeconomic change. In addition, it enables us to better comprehend the cause and effect of financialisation.

The outline of the book

The structure of this book is organised as follows: Chapter 1 delves into Veblen's most important conceptual contributions to evolutionary macroeconomics. The analysis begins with Veblen's cultural, holistic theorisation of the evolution of capital from industrial to business capital. Veblen brings to the fore, the role that pecuniary and emulation instincts have in institutionalising predatory habits and routines and fraudulent activities that destabilise financial markets and damages industrial processes. I highlight the significance of the cultural complexity of various processes of development and mutation of pecuniary habits of thought and routines that impose upon the macro-system certain rules that govern its change. Attention is paid to corporation finance as a process of institutional adaptation of the financial markets to business principles; and, especially, to Veblen's cultural 'financial instability hypothesis', which elucidates how the growth of pecuniary finance activates endogenous processes of fragile and unsustainable leverage structures, speculation and manipulation thereby inducing fragility and instability and debt-deflation processes. Lastly, Veblen's analysis of the cultural and pecuniary nature of effective demand and of liquidity allocation and income distribution is being demonstrated, since it is a fundamental element of his scrutiny of economic growth and business cycle.

Chapter 2 addresses Veblen's vision of economic policy from two angles. The first angle pays attention to Veblen's 'pessimistic bias' that arises from his 'financial macro-sociology', which contextualises the adaptation of economic policy-making to predatory and emulation instincts and financial institutions. It is pointed out that Veblen's scepticism revolved around the possibility of reversing reforms and policy interventions that institutionalise the vested interests of the elite of business and finance. The second angle places attention on Veblen's institutional reforms and fiscal and monetary policy interventions necessary for building of a more stable, efficient and humane capitalist order. I underline that Veblen's economic policy vision entails a continuous conflict between social forces that have vested interests in tangible investment, employment, industrial efficiency and the serviceable output produced, and social forces which have vested interests in making pecuniary profits in financial markets from intangible investment, speculation, manipulation, predatory and fraudulent practices and pecuniary efficiency.

Chapter 3 draws attention to Minsky's evolutionary macro-vision of his 'Wall Street' paradigm of capitalism. The analysis exposes three of the building blocks of Minsky's system of thought, which systematise his significant contribution to evolutionary macroeconomics. First, his Schumpeterian evolutionary outlook integrates financial entrepreneurship, innovation and competition with creative destruction processes in financial markets explaining fluctuations in employment, income and prices. Second, his 'financial instability hypothesis' illustrates the destabilising impact of speculative and Ponzi leverage and liability structures and failed margins of safety on the financial and macroeconomic systems. Attention is paid to Minsky's 'two price systems' that establish micro-meso-macro foundations to comprehend the coordination failure between cash inflow and cash outflow and the imperative role of insolvency. Third, his visualisation of the impact that fragile financial processes, unstable financial markets and income distribution exert on the financial structure of effective demand and on macroeconomic evolution.

Chapter 4 is devoted to Minsky's evolutionary approach to macroeconomic policy. The analysis underlines that Minsky's approach emanates from his institution-specific conceptualisation of the 'Wall Street' model of a capitalist economy; and that this approach has been heavily influenced from Keynes's political economy. Attention is placed on Minsky's suggestion that the inherent instability of financial markets and the cash dynamics of speculative and Ponzi position-making operations and failed margins of safety should be acknowledged as a first principle of institutional reforms and stabilisation policies. I elucidate that Minsky's 'financial instability hypothesis' and his 'two price systems' contextualise the evolving nature of the institutions of Big Government and Big Bank. Governments must use counter-cyclical targeted deficits to put a floor on the decline of effective demand and thus on current output prices so as to stabilise aggregate profits. The use of 'employer of last resort' programs is an institutional means for capitalist economies to endorse tight full employment and social cohesion. Finally, it is argued that, for Minsky, evolutionary central banking should apply qualitative monetary policy through discount window procedures and lender-of-last-resort interventions to smooth financing and funding of asset positions targeting the detection and eradication of speculative and Ponzi leverage structures.

Chapter 5 argues that the recontextualisation of modern macroeconomics becomes dependent upon its culturalisation. The analysis presents major concepts and principles of an evolutionary, holistic approach to macroeconomics. The main point of this approach is the need for scrutinising the cultural and financial aspects of processes of variation, selection and dispersion of habits of thought and routines in industry, business and banking. These processes are hypothesised to drive micro-meso-macro co-evolutionary structures of income and cash flows that govern macroeconomic change. Evolutionary financial macroeconomics focuses on the impact that the prevailing habits of thought and routines have on industrial efficiency, pecuniary efficiency, waste, effective demand, employment and growth. Yet, it is argued that the building of a macroeconomic safety net and the implementation of an evolutionary targeting fiscal policy and central banking appear to be critical for the establishment of a workmanship-led regime to promote full employment, financial stability and social provisioning.

The epilogue provides some general conclusions and paves the path for further research.

1 Veblen's Cultural Macroeconomics

Introduction

Veblen envisioned a cultural, holistic theory of macroeconomics.[1] This theory is unified within his general system[2] of social change where the actions and the behaviour of men are the subject matter. The evolution of the macro-system is conceptualised as a process of adaptation to a business environment that continuously and cumulatively changes under the influence of the evolving financial institutions. The evolution of financial institutions hinges on the natural selection of the fittest habits of thought and on the conflict between the instinct of workmanship and the pecuniary and emulative instincts.

In this chapter, I will trace the importance and enduring value of Veblen's insights that arguably form a valuable contribution to the building of evolutionary foundations for macroeconomics. My framework of interpretation underlines that Veblen introduced certain preconceptions and habits of thought that can recontextualise the subject matter of macroeconomic analysis.[3] I will argue that the essence of Veblen's macroeconomic theory is the elucidation of the cultural foundations of production, finance, prices, distribution, effective demand and economic growth, which differentiate the age of petty capitalist from the age of speculator, businessman and banker. Moreover, many of Veblen's insights could prove very valuable for those delving into the peculiar macroeconomic circumstances encompassing the financialised model of contemporary capitalism. Throughout his writings, over-leverage and deleverage, the recurring turbulence of financial markets, irrationalities of financing and funding, financial speculation and price manipulation as well as the depression, crisis and debt-deflation tendencies in credit-driven capitalist economies loom large as processes that determine the direction of macroeconomic change.[4] Of interest, too, is that Veblen's vision of the relation between the evolving financial institutions and the structure and functioning of the macro-system advances the comprehension of the course of financialisation.

The evolution of financial institutions

Veblen's macroeconomic theory is based on the Darwinian principles of variation, inheritance and selection and on the principle of cumulative causation.[5]

The essence of this theory is that a process of 'financial macro-institutional muta-tionism'[6] is the causal mechanism of macroeconomic change. The fundamental presumption is that the evolution of financial institutions is essential because it governs a capitalist economy's cyclical trends, growth and welfare potentials. The macroeconomy is a sub-system, along with other – i.e. financial, productive, dis-tribution – sub-systems, of the larger socio-cultural order in which it is embedded. As a part of a larger cultural complex, the macro-system is an ongoing process that reflects and affects the cumulative nature of the evolving socio-economic process.

In Veblen's cultural, holistic approach, macroeconomic analysis should not concentrate upon the behaviour of key macro-variables that detail a quantita-tive depiction of the macroeconomy. Rather, it should investigate macro-economic changes in light of the prevailing institutions in the business enterprise system. As I have argued elsewhere, (Argitis, 2016, p. 836):

> this is the reason that Veblen's conceptualisation does not focus entirely on the notions effective demand, overproduction, and the determinants of growth, of business cycles and employment. His aim was to elucidate the interaction between macro-evolution and the institutional adaptation of the business enterprise system.

Indeed, for Veblen, the proper subject of macroeconomics is the analysis of the cause and effect of the interconnectedness of the two most important institu-tions of capitalism namely the industrial system and the business enterprise. A point to stress is that Veblen placed emphasis on the interconnectedness between these two institutions because of their cultural dependence on the evolution of pecuniary habits of thought. Mitchell (1969) remarked the cultural difference between industry and business. He observed that, in Veblen's system, business enterprise is the art of making money, while the machine process is the modern art of making goods. In Veblen's (1919, p. 92) words,

> the business man's place in the economy of nature is to make money, not to produce goods. The production of goods is a mechanical process, incidental to the making of money; whereas the making of money is a pecuniary operation, carried on by bargain and sale, not by mechanical appliances and powers. The businessmen make use of the mechanical appliances and powers of the industrial system, but they make a pecuniary use of them.

This passage clearly displays Veblen's attention to the repercussions of the peculiar nature of business capital on the industrial system and on an economy's capacity to produce. On this ground, Mitchell (1969) underlined that Veblen's concern was to scrutinise how the business enterprise suppresses industrial effi-ciency, despite the fact that most economists, due to their habitual frame of mind, have viewed business enterprise as a great means for industrial develop-ment and growth.

To understand how industrial efficiency is suppressed, Veblen devoted his consideration to the reasons that make the macro-systems of a 'natural economy' and of a 'money economy' to be substantially dissimilar from the macro-system of a 'credit economy'. Veblen (1904) maintained that the most distinctive aspect of a money economy is the goods market, which, however, is no longer the dominant factor in a business enterprise economy since the capital market has taken the first place. In his frame of mind, the institutional distinction between a money economy and a credit economy discloses the dual nature of capital, which, in turn, reveals the adaptation processes of the business enterprise system to the evolving financial institutions. In the *Theory of Business Enterprise*, Veblen (1904) distinguished capital into physical or tangible and immaterial or intangible capital, and claimed that this distinction 'naturally' emanates from the evolution of capital from competitive proprietary business to large corporations. In many of his writings he demarcated the institutional connotations of the difference between tangible and intangible assets. Veblen (1919, pp. 69–70) endorsed that

> tangible assets, it appears, are such assets as represent the earning-capacity of any mechanically productive property; whereas intangible assets represent assured income which cannot be assigned to any specific material factor as its productive source. Intangible assets are the capitalised value of income not otherwise accounted for. Such income arises out of business relations rather than out of industry; it is derived from advantages of salesmanship, rather than from productive work.

The distinction between tangible and intangible capital is the origin of the division between the industrial and the business spheres of an economy. Veblen defined industry as the older order of capital that was principally identified in the form of machine processes. These processes generated income creation and distribution procedures, while their aim was the satisfaction of human needs. A point worth emphasising is that Veblen habitually used the concept of industry to refer to technology and its decisive role in growth dynamics as well as in social change. In contrast, he defined business as the processes of accumulating intangible assets and as procedures of market valuation and revaluation of tangible and intangible capital as putative earning-capacity. He envisaged intangible assets to represent no actual input to the produced output of goods and services but only a powerful claim to the distribution of the product surplus on property grounds, which appears to be institutionally legitimate.

Veblen used the distinction between industry and business to decode the causes of macroeconomic evolution. Veblen (1904, p. 18) originally visualised macroeconomic order and change to depend on

> the keeping of the balance in the comprehensive machine process of industry (which) is a matter of the gravest urgency if the productive mechanism is to proceed with its work in an efficient manner, so as to avoid idleness, waste, and hardship.

This passage displays that economic growth and macroeconomic change are hypothesised to hinge upon the accumulation of tangible capital, industrial efficiency and waste. Notably, the fact that Veblen concluded that there is an inverse relationship between industrial efficiency and waste. Nonetheless, industrial efficiency is not an ordinary condition of the business enterprise system. Veblen (1904, p. 17) recognised that

> a disturbance at any point, whereby any given branch of industry fails to do its share in the work of the system at large, immediately affects the neighbouring or related branches which come before or after it in the sequence, and is transmitted through their derangement to the remoter portions of the system.

Veblen seemed to suppose that macroeconomic order relies on an uninterrupted interchange of the various industrial processes. Seen from another angle, Veblen hypothesised that the growth dynamics of the multifaceted technological structure of the business enterprise system depend upon the harmony of the inter-industrial relations. But, Veblen proclaimed that industrial disorder is the most characteristic feature of the business enterprise system. This key assertion allowed him to surmise that the macro-system will tend to constantly operate below its full productive capacity. For Veblen, an economy's actual growth rate is very likely to be constantly below its potential growth rate.

He diagnosed as a possible reason for this macroeconomic underperformance the failure of businessman to function as a decisive factor in the management of the various industrial plants and processes, and in the supervision of the interstitial adjustments of the system. Besides, he remarked that such a failure is larger when technological progress is faster and the industrial system is more complex. After that, Veblen went deeper and scrutinised the causes of industrial disorder in light of the institutional structure of a real-world credit economy. In this regard, he underlined that any branch of industry, which inevitably enters in economy's credit system, is a complex bargaining process of money contracts, purchase and sale of goods and services and assets and goods prices. Furthermore, he upheld that the credit system is a structure of pecuniary transactions which, in Veblen's (1904, p. 27) words, "take place at the hands of the businessmen and are carried on by them for business ends, not for industrial ends". This division between industrial and pecuniary transactions was fundamental to his macro-vision. The reason is that this division qualified him to argue that the performance of the macro-system depends on the co-evolution between industrial and pecuniary processes that generates economic and pecuniary values, respectively.

Veblen (1901; 1908b) visualised the economic values as the real or tangible values, which are created by industrial processes and industrial employment. Economic values are commodities or services that accomplish personal and social needs. In contrast, pecuniary or market values are the final products of the business system and of pecuniary employment. Gruchy (1967, p. 108) marked out that pecuniary values are exchange values derived by market forces.

At bottom these pecuniary values are psychological rather than substantial, and consequently they have all the variability that goes with psychological phenomena. Unlike economic values which rest on material circumstances reducible to objective terms of mechanical, chemical, and psychological effect, pecuniary values rest on the uncertain foundation of vendibility.

In Veblen's system, vendibility means the competence of a product to bring pecuniary profit to businessman. Gruchy (1967) observed that vendibility is a matter of pecuniary serviceability, which might vary not in harmony with material serviceability or social utility, but in accordance with changes in mass or crowd psychology. These psychological changes are apparent mostly in periods of panic and speculation when there are significant discrepancies between economic and pecuniary values. In this regard, Mitchell (1969, p. 633) pointed out that

the commodities which are highly vendible may not be goods which are highly serviceable. Thus, the modern system of putting business in control of industry involves a constant bias in the direction of turning out goods which are fitted primarily to catch the purchaser's eye and appeal to his monetary desire rather than things which really gratify human wants.

In Veblen's theorising, as Gruchy (1967) argued, sometimes there is a high degree of coincidence between these two types of values that implies a harmonious relation. When this happens, pecuniary values are rough depictions of economic values. But there are also times when discrepancies between the streams of economic and pecuniary values prevent the latter from being ample measures of economic values. In this context, Veblen's macroeconomic scrutiny was directed to illuminate why there is not a permanent coincidence between economic and pecuniary values and whether it is feasible for the difference between them to diminish. It is worth noting that the institutional distinction between economic and pecuniary values crystallises the formation of Veblen's preconception concerning the repercussions of the institution of credit system for economic growth and community's welfare. In so doing, Veblen thoroughly researched the macroeconomic ramifications of the liquidity allocation and distribution inefficiencies that depict the business enterprise system. For Veblen (1919, pp. 92–93)

the highest achievement in business is the nearest approach to getting something for nothing. What any given business concern gains must come out of the total output of productive industry, of course; and to that extent any given business concern has an interest in the continued production of goods. But the less any given business concern can contrive to give for what it gets, the more profitable its own traffic will be. Business success means getting the best of the bargain.

The institutional reasoning behind Veblen's argument is that the structure and functioning of the business and financial systems engender pecuniary habits of thinking. The latter cumulatively and selectively become customary and eventually come to form the institutional setting which governs the structure of industrial, financial and distribution relations. Habits of mind, conventions and customs of conduct are passed on to the other sub-systems of an economy through adaptive processes in financial contracts and arrangements in business traffic. However, as Rutherford (1984) denoted, institutions are also themselves habits and routines that influence the process of selection. The consequences of the prevailing institutional setting are further strengthened because of financial innovations that activate new processes of competition and imitation for pecuniary gains.[7] According to Veblen, financial innovations restructure the credit relations and increase the degree of complexity and interrelatedness among an economy's various sub-systems. But, financial innovations are, mostly, pecuniary institutions that oxygenate from business principles and pecuniary values. They are introduced into the credit system on the basis of making pecuniary private gain and not of promoting employment, output and social gain. For Veblen (1919), the habitual frames of mind enable the owners and managers of any given concern or section of the business system to use financial innovations to make gains for themselves at the cost of the community. Community's welfare and the common good are best served by a higher production of economic values and by the efficient working of the industrial system at its full capacity. But, industrial efficiency is eroded by financial innovations, which, in conjunction with an increasing use of pecuniary debt, operate as an institutional channel that bequeaths certain habits and routines to the financing and funding processes in business and banking.

Financial markets, corporation finance and macroeconomic adaptation

The macroeconomic significance of pecuniary innovations and institutions is associated with the fact that they amplify the divergence between economic and pecuniary values. For Veblen, the adaptation process of the financial and macroeconomic structures is susceptible to institutions, which, in his system, are distinguished into two categories according to their purpose in economic activity. They are institutions of acquisition or of production, or as alternatively defined, institutions that serve the invidious or the non-invidious economic interests. The former category evolves around business principles, predatory instincts and the creation of pecuniary values, while the latter with machine processes and technology, the instinct of workmanship and the creation of economic values.

Veblen placed these two categories of institutions at the epicentre of his cultural theory of macroeconomics. As noted, he supposed that the structure of capital changes according to the evolving habitual frame of mind from the older order, where industry and business were unified, to the new order where they are separated, and, rather opposed. Veblen saw this separation as a systemic force that has induced significant structural and functioning modifications to various macro-sub-systems, i.e. investment spending, consumption spending, income distribution, technological relations, industrial structure, economic growth and livelihood. He continuously demarcated these macro-sub-systems as evolving cultural processes, which were parts of the co-evolution among industry, business and finance. He was groping towards a vision where macroeconomic change is anticipated in terms of the impact that the prevailing habits of thought, embodied in the evolving financial institutions, have on the separation of business from industry; and mostly on the speculative readjustments in the stock market valuation of business capital, which dishonour industrial capital and weaken businessmen's determination to serve economic growth and community's welfare.

As noted above, Veblen initially visualised the structure and functioning of macro-systems to rely on the complex technological interconnections of the industrial system, which rapidly grew on a large scale. His emphasis on the machine processes was crucially motivated by his belief in the decisive economic and social role of engineers, technicians and skilled workers. Veblen presumed that the principal aim of these social groups is to collectively coordinate all the sub-systems of the industrial sector so as to increase industrial efficiency and community's welfare. However, the consolidation of industrial and technological complexity prompted new organisational forms of power, which were further encouraged by institutional developments in the form of corporate finance and investment banking. One of the most useful of Veblen's macroeconomic obser-vations is that the adaptation of corporations and banks to the predominant busi-ness culture was a factor that increased variation and complexity within the industrial and financial systems, which fatefully reconfigure their co-evolution and symbiosis. For Veblen, the cultural co-evolution between industrial and financial systems is the basis for evaluating the quantitative change between pecuniary and economic values. At the micro-level, the institution that arranges this cultural relationship is the corporation finance. Mitchell (1969, p. 642) marked out that Veblen's perception of the conflict between the "cultural incidence of the machine process and the cultural incidence of business enterprise" standardises his institutional reasoning of the importance of corporation finance. Dirlam (1958, p. 199) underlined that corporation finance is "the distinguishing feature of Veblen's general theory of the economic process". Ganley (2004) and Wilson (2006) argued that Veblen's analysis of corporation finance is a major building block regarding his explanation of a finance-based capitalist economy. Raines and Leathers (2008) pinpointed that corporate finance connects banking and securities markets to the management of large corporations and the real economy. Argitis (2013a, p. 30) argued that corporation finance is a fundamental pillar of Veblen's macroeconomics, because it is "the institutional mechanism through which the financial markets adapt to the culture of the business enterprise system". Cor-poration finance integrates various institutions, such as industry, financial markets and the habitualisation process of business principles. This role eventuates from the capitalisation of large industrial corporations in the stock markets and of the con-tinuous and cumulative formation of leverage and liability structures which rest on credit. Capitalisation is a process of valuation and revaluation of business capital that institutionalises pecuniary habits in the trade of assets and the building of leverage. The macroeconomic effects are significant because, as I will argue below, capitalisation and leverage influence businessman's portfolio decisions to accumulate tangible and/or intangible assets, the allocation of liquidity by banks and ultimately the formation of sustainable or unsustainable liability structures.

In a credit economy, banks and financial markets, through complex financial processes and structures, channel liquidity, in the form of loans, bonds, stocks, etc., to corporations.[8] Businessmen and bankers build leverage structures when they make positions to get the largest pecuniary gain.[9] Leverage generates assets and liabilities and along with the allocation of liquidity by banks affects the complex interstitial relations of several branches of industry, the economy's financial structure and, in due course, the qualitative elements of the symbiosis and co-evolution between industrial and financial systems. This co-evolution involves debt contracts and financial arrangements for future performance and obligations that influence the industrial and financial order. For instance, if an industrial unit or branch does not have access to new liquidity lines or if it obtains less liquidity from what it needs to carry on planned investment and/or to fulfil financial commitments, then it is likely that it would fail to play its role in the complex industrial and financial structures. The result would be to disturb neighbouring or related industrial units and branches as well as their banks. Under such circumstances, financial and macroeconomic disorder and instability would prevail. Yet, output produced would be below the level that was expected and therefore debt commitments might not be fulfilled.

Veblen focused extensively on the misallocation of liquidity from the banking system and connected it to the habitual frame of mind of those engaged in the funding and financing routines in the business and banking sectors. By noting this principle, what seems to be crucial, in his viewpoint, is if the customary routines in banking promote the financing of new technological combinations in industrial processes, and the production of serviceable output, or not. Veblen seemed to endorse that a mechanism that efficiently allocates liquidity, among other technological and organisational factors, is decisive for the stability and the order of operational dealings and transactions among the several industrial branches, as well as for the industrial processes to be maintained, adjusted and readjusted. If the established routines in banking institutionalise lending norms and techniques that approve the financing of investment in tangible assets, the rate of economic growth will increase and accelerate. In contrast, if they approve the financing of intangible assets and conspicuous consumption, the rate of growth of serviceable output will drop. Therefore, financial institutions discipline the conditions that establish, or not, a well-performed and balanced industrial system. Furthermore, financial institutions are also important in the process of building sustainable, or not, asset and liability structures. The allocation of liquidity is vital for a corporation's recapitalisation. An uninterrupted refinancing of the inherited leverage prevents insolvency and bankruptcies that make the financial system fragile. Besides, it maintains the market value of tangible and intangible assets.

As stated, an efficient allocation of liquidity presumes banks to institutionalise financing routines that encourage investment in tangibles assets thereby promoting the instinct of workmanship. But, this presupposition contradicts with Veblen's pragmatism where business principles, ultimately, triumph as capital evolves. In his

Absentee Ownership and Business Enterprise in Recent Times, Veblen (1923) regarded corporate finance as a process that converts corporations and banks to pecuniary institutions that seek gains for building business capital in financial markets. Veblen drew attention to the predisposition of corporations and banks to stay away from machine processes and industrial production. Regarding this type of bias of corporations, in his *Theory of Business Enterprise*, Veblen (1904, p. 85) wrote that a corporation "is always a business concern, not an industrial appliance". Besides, Veblen (1904, pp. 36–37) upheld that

> the end of his (entrepreneur) endeavours is, not simply to effect an industrially advantageous consolidation, but to effect it under such circumstances of ownership as will give him control of large business forces or bring him the largest possible gains. The ulterior end sought is an increase of ownership, not industrial serviceability.

It is also worth noting that for Veblen, investment becomes a peculiar device for the businessman to curtail the processes of industry. For businessmen the motive is the pecuniary expediency of the evaluation of the production process in terms of the monetary gains from investment, not expediency in terms of serviceability to the community. However, Veblen perceived that disserviceability may well be capitalised as willingly as serviceability. He argued that the ownership of invested wealth affords a discretionary power to deprave industrial efficiency so as to make higher pecuniary profits and shares of ownership. These are the final goal of business and not the production of serviceable goods and the promotion of community's welfare. In Veblen's (1908b, pp. 104–105) words,

> investment is a pecuniary transaction, and its aim is pecuniary gain, -gain in terms of value and ownership. Invested wealth is capital, a pecuniary magnitude, measured in terms of value and determined in respect of its magnitude by a valuation which proceeds on an appraisement of the gain expected from the ownership of this invested wealth.

At this point, it is important to stress that corporate finance also establishes the cultural foundations for Veblen's effort to cast doubt upon the folklore of Political Economy. The latter postulates that corporations exert a creative force on productive industry, because, as Veblen (1923, p. 86) remarked, "it draws out of retirement many small accumulated hoards of savings, and so combines them and puts them to work when they would otherwise remain idle". Veblen fully rejected the presumption, which still holds in modern equilibrium macroeconomics and in the efficient financial market hypothesis, that savings create income as soon as they are invested and capitalised by corporations. He approved that this assertion relies on the preconception that the financing of corporations through funds received from the financial markets adds to material equipment or industrial output. Veblen (1923, p. 86) proclaimed that "this faith in the creative efficiency of capital funds and capitalised savings is one of the axioms of the business community". The savings and liquidity which are hypothesised to be drawn out and mobilised by corporations in fact are held out in the form of funds and of records of ownership. The customary pecuniary habits of thought in the corporate sector are so that liquidity is probably not to be used for new investment in tangible assets, but for carrying a higher scale of leverage that accelerates business concentration in stock markets and increases the share of ownership.

Similarly, in the banking business, liquidity may not always be used for financing new industrial combinations promoting technological progress and economic growth. The growth of financial markets and financial innovations bears a variety of new pecuniary investment opportunities that might shift the point of businessmen's and bankers' concern away from investing in gainful industrial combinations towards investing in more profitable financial assets. The growth of financial markets enlarges the capability of businessmen and bankers to disassociate their profits and social status from the discipline to improve industrial efficiency and serviceability. But this choice disturbs the efficient interaction of the various machine processes that structure the industrial system. To businessmen, bankers and financiers productive lending and serviceability are not their key goal. Their aim is to make pecuniary gains;[10] the means of achieving this is the development of various financial innovations, techniques and practices.

As financial markets gained ground, it is sensible to argue that finance may become more amenable to pecuniary habits of thought and speculative routines. This process accelerates the cultural adjustment of the industrial and macroeconomic systems to business values and principles. Besides, this outcome increases the conflict between the habits of mind conducive to industrial efficiency and those conducive to pecuniary efficiency. The separation between pecuniary and economic values escalates as liquidity is provided along with business and not industrial and technological principles. In this regard, Veblen (1904, p. 66) wrote that

> as the machine process conditions the growth and scope of industry, and as its discipline inculcates habits of thought suitable to the industrial technology, so the exigencies of ownership condition the growth and aims of business, and the discipline of ownership and its management inculcates views and principles (habits of thought) suitable to the work of business traffic.

Veblen's 'financial instability hypothesis'

One of Veblen's most impressive conceptions is that in the business enterprise system liquidity is supplied and leverage and liability structures are built along with business and not industrial principles. This conception contextualises Veblen's 'financial instability hypothesis' (from now on VFIH). This hypothesis advances his cultural macroeconomic theory and invigorates its enduring value as long as finance capitalism is the prevailing economic and social order. The insight that founds VFIH is that severe competition among organisations increases leverage beyond the limit required by the amount of the produced serviceable goods. Veblen envisaged debt creation as a process that occurs when bankers postulate that corporations' good-will[11] and future profits create the liquidity flows that are necessary to fulfil the payments due to debts and to avoid crutches and bankruptcy. Moreover, he remarked that bankers' experience on the subject of refinancing an inherited debt structure and on the quality of good-will formulates their anticipation of corporations' solvency risk. In this respect, Veblen (1904, p. 101) claimed that

> the greater part of the advances made by banking houses, for instance, rest on the lender's presumptive ability to pay eventually, on demand or at maturity, any claims that may in the course of business be presented against the lender on account of the advances made by him.

For Veblen, in a credit-driven economy, solvency is decisive for organisations' capacity to refinance and validate inherited debt-structures.

However, the 'captains of industry and finance' make positions in financial markets and create asset and liabilities structures in order to make pecuniary gains. Veblen identified this habit as a factor that eventually renders the leverage and liability structures of banks and corporations unsustainable. The reason is that if the accumulated debt increases business capital, and not the industrial capital, the quality of leverage may deteriorate. Loans that expand business capital represent no material capital. It is in reality, fictitious industrial capital. Veblen drew attention to the point that non-productive leverage is used by managers to induce an enthusiastic environment for corporation's capacity to be straightforwardly recapitalised in stock markets. Nevertheless, unproductive leverage cannot stimulate aggregate productivity of industry. Yet, at the macro-level, unproductive leverage worsens an economy's actual and potential growth rates and capacity to generate sustainable income and liquidity flows. In addition, pecuniary leverage upsurges business capital and increases, cumulatively, the market value of an organisation's collateral that can be, speculatively, utilised for new position-making and refinancing. Veblen also pinpointed the possibility of the process of leverage creation boosting the price of industrial products. The latter, in turn, is likely to stimulate industrial production. For Veblen, this expansionary impact of leverage on prices and industrial production is essentially psychological and significant mostly in brisk times. Pecuniary over-leverage is habitual during the prosperity phase of the business cycle and it is eventually destabilising.

Veblen endorsed the mixture of pecuniary recapitalisation and unproductive leverage as an endogenous mechanism of financial fragility and instability. His analysis placed emphasis on the liquidity, income and distribution effects of pecuniary leverage. It was argued that businessmen decide to increase leverage when they expect a substantial difference between the cost of a leverage structure and the gross increase of gains to be made by its use. This difference largely depends on the productive or less productive use of credit, which will increase or diminish the output of industry, and, so, will affect the aggregate earnings of corporations. As capitalisation goes on and liquidity is likely not to be used to finance the growth of the aggregate industrial-productive equipment, industrial efficiency, output and the aggregate gross earnings decline. The less productive the use of leverage is, the higher the negative effect on gross earnings and on net (after interest) profits is. This negative profit effect jeo-pardises the capability of businessmen to fulfil debt obligations, thereby raising the solvency risk for corporations and banks.

VFIH configures a cultural theorisation between solvency, financial fragility and the discrepancy between business and industrial capital. The dynamics of VFIH arise from the leverage and liability creation processes, which rest on the value of business capital as expressed in terms of the value of collateral and of the expected profits. The creation of leverage proceeds so long as there is not a negative price effect on the cumulative growth of capitalised values. This then presupposes the existence of reliable expectations regarding the market value of collateral. Veblen understood and endorsed the importance of the putative stability of the money value of the capitalised industrial material for businessmen and bankers, since it crucially matters for organisations' recapitalisation and adaptation. This insight discloses, as argued below, the destabilising effects of the institutions of price manipulation and fraud. Furthermore, the putative stability of the money value of collateral of the capitalised industrial structures is cumulatively augmented by the process of capitalisation itself and the pecuniary supply of credit. In this context, the creation of leverage has a pecuniary character. For this reason, the likelihood of the inherited liability structure to be unsustainable is high.

If an increase in the leverage and liability structures of corporations and banks is substantially large in proportion to the productive capacity of industry, the dis-crepancy between the money value of collateral and corporation's actual earning-capacity might also be substantially extensive. For Veblen, this is likely to induce a forced recapitalisation of corporations, bringing their nominal aggregate business capital in accordance with the actual earning-capacity generated by the aggregate industrial capital. Any such recapitalisation reduces the quality of banks' balance sheets, thus activating insolvency, problems of creditworthiness and bankruptcies. Veblen (1904) contemplated two methods of rating the value of collateral,[12] which contextualise his preconception of the cultural basis of solvency and cred-itworthiness. The first method connects the market value of collateral with the growth of leverage. The latter is related to the putative stability of the money value of the capitalised industrial material, which is cumulatively augmented by the growth of leverage itself. In this method, any variation in the market price of financial assets is crucial because it determines the confidence of recapitalisation and the stability of the market value of collateral. The second method emphasises on the fact that the money value of collateral is the capitalised value of good-will computed on the basis of the discrepancy between actual and presumptive earn-ing-capacity. This discrepancy, Veblen argued, depends on goods price, produc-tion cost and effective demand. But, as shown below, these micro-macro variables eventually hinge on the prevailing habits and routines in industry and finance. Veblen (1904) argued that these two methods must overlap in order for capitali-sation to be effective and for corporations to open new lines of refinancing.

Mitchell (1969) highlighted the overlapping between the two methods of rating the value of business capital. Yet, he asserted that in Veblen's vision, the evolution of the business enterprise system is ultimately governed by the interaction between recapitalisation and the expected stream of prospective profits of the capital stock underlying the revaluation of financial assets. In this regard, Veblen explicitly espoused that if business capital grows faster than industrial capital, a discrepancy arises between the expected pecuniary profits and the actual earning-capacity. If there is a discrepancy between the computed results given by the two ratings, then a recapitalisation will take effect on the ground of corporation's computed earning-capacity. In this framework, it is fully understood, indeed, why Veblen devoted considerable attention to technology and industrial efficiency as factors that eventually discipline the revaluation of business capital and the macro-dynamics of the business enterprise system.

It is worth noting that the earning-capacity being the centre for the revaluation of the capitalisation of the assets bought and sold, is not the actual earning-capacity, but the presumptive future earning-capacity. This insight brought the concept of uncertainty to the fore in Veblen's macroeconomics. In his viewpoint, variations in anticipation of future events induce fluctuations in capital markets and probably in the valuation of corporate capital.[13] However, the effective recapitalisation of business capital is vulnerable to a perpetual process of valuation and revaluation of corporation's properties – tangible and intangible – on the basis of its actual earning-capacity and, as Veblen (1904, p. 149) noticed, on "folk psychology". Veblen marked out the importance of the most elusive and intangible assets in forming the expectation about the capitalised good-will. He denoted the fact that these types of assets are not serviceable to growth and community's welfare, but only owners' vested interests. They are subject to market fluctuations and to the manoeuvres of businessmen and bankers. Besides, the effective recapitalisation, and, hence, the stability of the market value of collateral, appears to vary in line with investor's confidence about the solvency risk of corporations and banks. If financial markets experience a discrepancy between actual and presumptive profits and/or a decrease in market value of collateral, then recapitalisation interrupts, solvency collapses, and a period of liquidation and debt-deflation would probably begin. Veblen argued that few branches and firms might fall into this position especially during a period of phenomenally brisk times, where their liabilities become bad debts. When such financial conditions prevail, a corporation may be forced to deliver its output at lower, than the expected, prices.

The consequence is that financial markets might evaluate capitalisation as excessive because of negative expectations about corporation's earning-capacity. For Veblen, solvency concerns arise when debtors are incapable of meeting their obligations out of current earnings. If the claims against debtors are pressed, they have no recourse but to proceed with practices of liquidation through forced sales or bankruptcy. Both effects, especially if they are large, are disastrous for an economy's financial structure. Veblen (1904, pp. 204–205) wrote that

> when such a situation has come, all that is required to bring on the general catastrophe is that some considerable creditor find out that the present earning-capacity of his debtor will probably not warrant the capitalisation on which his collateral is appraised. In self-defence he must decline the extension of a loan, and forced liquidation must follow.

If liquidation begins, then the prices of goods and assets and the profits will decrease throwing firms into the class of insolvent. Such an effect would stimulate the readjustment of a corporation's capitalisation and good-will. Another plausible consequence would be the insolvency of the banks that had involved in unwise lending to insolvent industrial enterprises. It is impressive that Veblen (1904, p. 205) outlined certain liquidity preconditions for an economy to avoid insolvency and financial fragility and instability. He claimed that

> the abruptness of the recapitalisation and of the redistribution of ownership involved in a period of liquidation may be greatly mitigated ... by a judicious leniency on the part of the creditors or by a well-advised and discreetly weighted extension of credit by the government to certain sections of the business community.

Concluding, VFIH elucidates that macroeconomic order and stability presume the order and stability of the financial system. But, financial order and stability needs income creation and distribution processes that sustain an effective demand up to the level that absorbs the maximum of serviceable output produced. On the other hand, macroeconomic order and stability leans on the capacity of the financial system to bear the liquidity flows that sustain the solvency of corporations' leverage and liability structures and recapitalisation. In Veblen's system, the quality and sustainability of the financial structure of effective demand mirror the effectiveness of the above-mentioned income and liquidity creation processes. In this regard, financial institutions and financial markets are essential because they are cultural processes that valuate and revaluate pecuniary assets, thus influencing macroeconomic change that comes about as a readjustment process of the financial structure of effective demand. As a result, coherence between the macroeconomic and financial systems is uncertain and susceptible to the predominant pecuniary habits of thought and routines. On these terms, Veblen proclaimed the pecuniary character of macroeconomic evolution and the cultural foundations of his macroeconomic theory. Financial fragility and instability, debt-deflation and depression have a substantial role in his macro-vision for the reason that they are fundamental constitutes of the pecuniary culture of the business enterprise system. Ultimately, Veblen visualised the evolution of business principles and habits as the most decisive factors behind the co-evolution among industry, finance and the macroeconomy.

The institutions of manipulation and fraud

Introspecting macroeconomic evolution on the basis of capital valuation by investors into a credit-driven and debt-accumulated economy, Veblen outlined the role of the institutions of manipulation and fraud. He perceived these institutions as principles of pecuniary success on the matters of solvency and creditworthiness in the realms of recapitalisation and refinancing. Given the growth of financial markets, Veblen underlined that for leveraged organisations, the evaluation of solvency by investors shifted from the cost of production and the prices of goods to the earning-capacity as a going concern. Yet, he maintained that solvency and intangible good-will rather than tangible assets are the major factors that form investor's expectations of corporations' earning-capacity. Note that intangible assets are non-serviceable capital spending and hence do not add potentialities to corporations' productive capacity. In aggregate terms, intangible assets improve neither the competence of the industrial system, nor does the community's welfare.

Furthermore, as noted, Veblen asserted that the evaluation of solvency and recapitalisation does not depend on the past or actual earning-capacity, but on the putative earning-capacity, which, for a given business capital, is calculated by investor's presumptions about the future actual earning-capacity. The latter is derived by the accumulated tangible assets and the competence of a corporation's machine process. However, the actual earning-capacity is implausible to be known in advance, as expectations about the future are vastly conjectural. Tugwell (1939) and Vining (1939) pinpointed that, in Veblen's system, forecasts are volatile because the future is uncertain and there is too much optimism in business decisions principally in periods of inflationary and speculative prosperity. Veblen seemed to endorse that in an uncertain world, the willingness to lever or debt-finance positions in tangible and, especially, in intangible capital assets depends upon investors' credible evaluation of corporation's solvency and earning-capacity. Unanticipated variations in prospective industrial profits engender fluctuations in putative profits. Frequent discrepancies between actual and putative earning-capacity alter confidence on organisations' liability structure and creditworthiness. This then disrupts refinancing, recapitalisation and investment decisions. Bolbol and Lovewell (2001) exemplified Veblen's distinction between putative and actual earning-capacity within, what they outlined as, Veblen's q theory. They pointed out that Veblen's q exposes the impact that the valuation of a corporation's capitalisation causes on corporate and industrial structures. Bolbol and Lovewell (2001, p. 528) claimed that Veblen's q is determined "independently of monetary policy and the state of productivity of the company" and that it is predisposed to stock market manipulation so as to produce rapid turnover of corporations control.

In my point of view, VFIH and Veblen's q theory expose the cause that renders the elite of business and finance amenable to manipulation of prices, and, as Hake (2007) observed, of expectations. The idea is that the elite of business and finance intentionally mislead investors on the subject of the discrepancy between corporations' putative and actual earnings. The reason is that they want to control the prices of assets and to manage the market value of collateral and good-will. In this regard, Veblen (1904, pp. 160–161) marked out that

> the stock market interest of those men who have the management of industrial corporations is a wide and multifarious one. It is not confined to the profitable purchase and sale of properties whose management they may have in hand. They are also interested in making or marring various movements of coalition or reorganisation, and to this ulterior end it is incumbent on them to manipulate

securities with a view to buying and selling in such a manner as to gain control of certain lines of securities.

In a similar vein, Veblen incorporated into his vision the manipulation of the goods price. Price-cutting strategies that consolidate the monopoly power of a corporation, fraud and false news about the quality of products, etc., are adopted by managers to affect the market valuation of a corporation's expected profits and hence the market value of its shares, collaterals and solvency. Henry (2012, p. 997) emphasised that for Veblen the two most noteworthy categories of fraud regards "the inflation of the value of capital relative to capital stock and the use of good-will to institutionally shift income (profits) to firms, most successful in engaging in fraudulent behavior". Argitis (2016) underlined that successful fraudulent activities secure pecuniary profit in balance sheets and, therefore, misinform investors about the sustainability of corporations' liability structure. Manipulation and fraud institutionalise the interests and predatory instincts of the elite of business and finance who attempt to emulate successfully. Accordingly, manipulation and fraud may become a customary operating procedure of significant concern in business traffic.

A generalisation of Veblen's view could be made so as to include the manipulation of monetary and financial factors, i.e. interest rates, bond prices. Banks, investment banks and other financial institutions are predatory in nature. Argitis (2016, p. 842) argued, the manipulation of monetary and financial variables implies the "manipulation of economic conditions that shape expectations, consumption, investment decisions, government spending processes, and effective demand". Misinformation of investors might emanate from their attempts to manipulate expectations about the solvency and the quality of balance sheets, so as to communicate confidence in their reputation and capacity to meet debt commitments and to secure pecuniary profits. Argitis (2013a) pinpointed that businessmen and bankers may manage prices according to the quality of their leverage and liability structures. Banks and corporations with manipulated capitalisation appear to be successful and financially solvent organisations, and, hence, it is more likely for them to have access to new liquidity lines in financial markets. Manipulation and fraudulent practices give wrong information and create illusions and biased solvency rankings. But, the evaluation of solvency on the basis of the manipulated quality of balance sheets that designates the success of businessmen to increase leverage is to a certain degree intangible and elusive.

This effect, as Lawson and Lawson (1990) and Raines and Leathers (1992; 2008) acknowledged, relies on the pace of financial product innovations, e.g. securitisation, futures and interest rate swaps. Pecuniary financial innovations increase speculative liquidity and together with processes of imitation and routinisation cultivate conditions for bubbles. Moreover, emulation motivates businessmen and bankers to struggle for social distinction and reputation. The business culture is such that higher leverage might not be used to finance new industrial processes and to create jobs, but as a symbol of economic and social power, status and prestige. In addition, successful emulation engenders more severe manipulation and fraudulent practices to further advance corporations' and banks' biased solvency and access to new liquidity lines, regardless of their actual solvency and credit risk. In this manner, predatory and emulation instincts drive businessmen and bankers towards over-leverage and the building of, probably unsustainable, liability structures. Sooner or later, the manipulated discrepancy between putative and actual profits becomes known. Changes in expectations about the fragility of balance sheets in combination with a debt structure that generate commitments that cannot be fulfilled might bring about insolvency, deleverage and, ultimately, debt-deflation.

Veblen drew particular attention to the idea that investors' anticipation of the actual earning-capacity of a capital may differ substantially from the one that managers know. He espoused that outsiders' information does not coincide with that of insiders. In particular, in the following passage Veblen (1904, p. 156) indicated that expectations and presumptions "will vary from one man to the next, since they proceed on an imperfect, largely conjectural, knowledge of present earning-capacity and on the still more imperfectly known future course of the goods market and of corporate policy". Bolbol and Lovewell (2001) argued that imperfect information and knowledge render objective values implausible in stock markets.[14] As a result, managers, whose valuation of earning-capacity is reflected in the denominator of Veblen's q, manipulate investor's anticipation of the putative earning-capacity, which is reflected in the numerator. Furthermore, Bolbol and Lovewell (2001) remarked that, in Veblen's system, manipulation makes stock markets more volatile and speculative because prices do not reflect valuations that depend on economic fundamentals, such as tangible assets and actual profits, but on spurious foundations, such as good-will and intangible assets.

Raines and Leathers (1996; 2000) accentuated that Veblen's exposition of the processes by which stock prices are formed and of how they determine expectations about a corporation's putative earning-capacity is more complicated than the conventional fundamental value theory. The reason is that Veblen incorporated into his vision a strong psychological factor.[15] The argument of Raines and Leathers is based on Veblen's statement upon folk psychology. Veblen (1904, p. 149) upheld that fluctuations in the amount of capital in stock markets

> proceed on variations of confidence on the part of the investors, on current belief as to the probable policy or tactics of the businessmen in control, on forecasts as to the seasons and the tactics of the guild of politicians, and on the indeterminable, largely instinctive, shifting movements of public sentiment and apprehension. So that under modern conditions the magnitude of the business capital and its mutations from day to day are in great measure a question of folk psychology rather than of material fact.

But if stock prices are heavily influenced by psychological forces and imperfect information and knowledge rather than by rational decisions taken under perfect information and knowledge of actual earning-capacity, then the stock markets, as Bolbol and Lovewell (2001) and Raines and Leathers (1996; 2000) argued, cannot be efficient markets. In this framework, Veblen's q is instrumental in understanding business behaviour, because it deliberately merges pecuniary habits and routines with intangible capital, corporation's good-will and solvency. In addition, as argued below, it discloses the endogenous desta-bilising forces of the business enterprise system, as a higher q may be a warning sign of declining growth of tangible investment.

In other words, a higher value of Veblen's q signals certain distribution and welfare effects. Business and financial leaders could exploit changes in asset prices to increase their speculative gains. In addition, manipulation and fraud boost pecuniary efficiency and augment the ownership of property for the elite of busi-ness and finance'. However, their interests need coincide neither with the interest of corporations[16] and banks, nor with the interest of the community. As noted, the interest of the community is served by higher industrial efficiency, low prices and the maximum growth of serviceable goods, which, however, are not portrayed by manipulation and fraud. Veblen (1904, pp. 158–159) marked that in the industrial order of a money economy, the discretionary control of the production process was in the hands of the owners whose interests are different from community's interests.

> But under the regime of the more adequately developed credit economy, with vendible corporate capital, the interest of the men who hold the discretion in industrial affairs is removed by one degree from the concerns under their management, and by two degrees from the interests of the community at large.

Concluding, in credit-driven economies, manipulation and fraud are habits and routines customised by the elite of business and finance to control changes in prices so as to manage the value and stability of pecuniary wealth and good-will and the quality of balance sheets. As such they are part of organisations' recapitalisation and refinancing process. But the higher they are used, the higher financial fragility and society's loss of welfare are.

Over-leverage, deleverage and debt-deflation

By putting emphasis on solvency and unsustainable income and cash flow creation processes that generate financial fragility, VFIH uncovers the debt-deflation and depression tendencies that finance capitalism generates. Moreover, the emphasis of Veblen's q on the ratio between tangible and intangible assets exposes the dynamics of VFIH, which figure out a cultural structure to examine business cycles and depression tendencies. In my viewpoint, the enduring value of VFIH is the depiction of the peculiar and elusive character of solvency as a basis for evaluating the quality of organisations' leverage and liability structures, creditworthiness and recapitalisation. Of interest, too, is that solvency depends on the vendibility of capital, tangible and intangible and good-will.

Veblen's exploration of financial fragility and instability concentrates emphasis on financial commitments derived by changes in nominal and real debt burdens that come about, mostly, during periods of prosperity. Over-leverage, deleverage, insufficient demand and deflation are the cause and effect of financial fragility and instability. The central tenet of Veblen's analysis is that over-indebtedness induces high rates of speculative inflation, higher pecuniary gains and unsustainable debt commitments. The latter is the result of the pecuniary restructuring of capital due to the accumulation of intangible assets. Deleverage and insufficient demand make nominal debts and leverage structures unbearable real debt burdens and unsustainable liability structures that eventually cause liquidation and deflation.

More specifically, Veblen's q presumes that the evaluation of a corporation's capitalisation, solvency and vendibility, as communicated and evaluated in financial markets, does not reflect the actual value of industrial equipment and a corporation's productive capacity. The evaluation varies along with fluctuations in the concerned earning-capacity. As I mentioned earlier, the differences between putative and actual earning-capacity, which determine the medium-term and long-term quality of leverage, hinge on the balance between tangible and intangible assets. An increase in the share of intangible assets to total assets compels divergences between economic and pecuniary values, which, in due course, erode confidence in the sustainability of a corporation's earning-capacity. The tangible capital in use yields the ordinary earning-capacity, which represents the state of the industrial arts, the utilisation of the productive capacity and the efficiency of the mechanical apparatus engaged in the production processes of goods and services. On the other hand, pecuniary profits, which come from speculative leverage and manipulation of prices, do not represent a return for any productive work. They emanate from immaterial dealings in financial markets and represent routinised business principles and pecuniary efficiency. Note that in Veblen's system, the market value of securities ultimately rests on the tangible assets of the good-will. What it is important in Veblen's analysis is that any asset, tangible or intangible, represents a claim to future income flows, including anticipated capital gains from rises in good and asset prices. Higher pecuniary profits and market value of collateral might create possibilities for effective recapitalisation and refinancing from new liquidity lines in financial markets, which increase organisations' leverage.

Nevertheless, as pecuniary profits increase and the putative earning-capacity is preserved, bankers and managers may be less willing to invest in tangible assets. They might be more enthusiastic to use their pecuniary wealth for increasing parasitic, non-productive spending, such as conspicuous consumption and investment in intangible assets. The end result of this behaviour is the restructure of private aggregate demand. The latter becomes more parasitic in the sense that it absorbs less from industry's serviceable output produced. This effect then damages industry's capacity to create actual profits from producing serviceable goods, as well as workers' capacity to earn wage-income from productive employment. Veblen's q involves that when the balance between tangible and intangible assets change, sooner or later, the anticipation of organisations' solvency by investors is likely to change. High q valuations signal that the intangible assets of good-will are collateralised by an increased volume of securities that might not be backed by actual tangible assets. Medlen (2003, p. 974) placed emphasis on Veblen's valuable distinction between the older industrial order and the credit-driven business order. In the former case, the accumulation of debt reflected industry's tangible asset base of inventories and plant. As collateral, this tangible asset base had a certain cost of production, which operated "as implicit floor under its valuation". This tangible relationship between the accumulated debt and the creation of assets mitigated the repercussions of a credit crisis, because the liquidation of inventories and plant was a potential source of liquidity flows that could be used to pay down the debt. In contrast, in modern business circumstances, leverage and securitisation have been grounded on the intangible assets of the good-will and on putative valuations of future profits that are not likely to be accurately measured. In addition, the financialisation of the business enterprise system and the broad use of the institutions of manipulation and fraud increase uncertainty over investor's confidence in the value of these intangible assets. Veblen (1923) was aware of the variability in the market value of these intangibles, as well as of the risk of a credit system collapse. He observed that this variability heavily relies on the discrepancies between organisation's putative and actual earning-capacities, which increase uncertainty. In Veblen's system, a higher value of q denotes higher securitisation and collateralisation of intangible assets with unsustainable and uncertain market valuation. Seen from another angle, a higher value of q possibly indicates higher solvency risk. Veblen condemned the collateralisation of securities that were not backed by actual tangible assets, because it increases the fragility of the credit structure. At this point, it is worthy to make a reference to Medlen's (2003) comment that overindebtedness and securitisation was the other side of the 'free income' that the upper class claim in the distribution of the product surplus. As argued below, the higher the level of 'free income' and intangible worth of the elite of business and finance, the higher the insufficient demand and the greater the portion of an economy's inherited debt not backed by actual tangible assets.

These potentials contextualise Veblen's endogenous mechanism of financial instability, which works as follows: the evolution of financial institutions cumulatively coerces the accumulation of intangible assets. This then erodes the sustainability of actual profits, the market value of collateral and, ultimately, organisations' solvency. But, solvency is an element of good-will and a guiding principle of corporations' recapitalisation and refinancing. For Veblen, the unconditional recapitalisation of good-will is a prerequisite for credit expansion and over-leverage. The manipulated putative earning-capacity misinforms investors about the quality of leverage and liability structures. The manipulation of the capitalised leverage induces biased solvency rankings, which increase the complexity of corporations and banks' financial structure, linkages and income and liquidity flows. The business culture is such that a higher Veblen's q communicates illusions to investors concerning the solvency and creditworthiness of organisations and their concrete capacity to meet debt obligations and refinance position-making. The higher the unproductive use of credit, the higher the manipulation and fraud might need to be for managers and investment bankers to succeed in emulation. The unpreventable accumulation of pecuniary profits and financial assets boosts the market value of collateral and escalates capitalisation in financial markets. Simultaneously, it further demoralises the growth of tangible assets and the creation of profits engendered by industrial processes. This structural imbalance upsurges the discrepancy between putative and actual profits activating solvency risk. Given the cultural setting and the inherited debt and liability structure, the selection of predatory and pecuniary financial innovations and institutions by the business and banking community would create possibilities for a liquidity crash and financial instability.

For Veblen, financial instability begins when solvency collapses stimulating deleverage and liquidity shortages. Liquidity is provided on the basis of the expected variations in the market price of goods and collateral. Veblen (1905, p. 461) asserted that prices are "a fact upon which the business community's hopes and fears center". Higher goods and assets prices, at least in important industrial branches, stimulate profits and the supply of liquidity, because of the higher market value of collateral. Veblen pinpointed that this chain of events follows the prosperity phase of the economic cycle. However, this chain of events is reversed when bankers' expectations change. A fall in stock market valuations decreases corporations' borrowing power and upsurges the burden of debt relative to the asset values of good-will. As the lower market value of good-will is incorporated into the solvency status of an organisation, the acceptable leverage ranking by banks might fall. Veblen proclaimed that when refinancing is interrupted, the solvency risk increases and investment falls. However, lower investment especially in tangible assets reduces both the actual and putative earning-capacity, which further increase the solvency risk. The structure of investment spending shows how cultural factors and financial routines in business and banking are interrelated and how the prevailing habits of thought, manipulation and pecuniary solvency affect the evolution of capital. In this context, any particular structure of private investment appears to be a cultural-financial singularity.

Veblen went deeper and scrutinised the financial and macroeconomic ramifications of insolvent leverage and liability structures. In his viewpoint, over-indebtedness activates two contradictory forces. It gives to businessmen, who compete for pecuniary gains, the means to cumulatively overinvest, mostly during business upturn. As noted above, the growing corporation is in a better position to negotiate with banks a higher leverage, thereby further increasing its capitalisation and the market value of collateral. An extensive use of credit is also expected to bring about a fall in goods price due to advances in industrial efficiency. However, these beneficial effects in terms of society's welfare are likely to reduce organisation's actual and expected earning-capacity. With actual profits falling short of the previously expected profits, the capitalised valuations of business assets pledged as collateral for new lines of liquidity falls too. As a result, corporations' good-will and solvency are jeopardised. In addition, falling profits in their turn impair the ability of businessmen to validate the quality of balance sheets and to accomplish contractual financial obligations. Accordingly, pecuniary and speculative over-leverage eventually triggers solvency and liquidity risks, which are likely to activate deleverage processes in banking and business sectors.

Deleverage begins when solvency collapses because of insufficient aggregate demand and rising wages that eradicate business profits. Yet, Veblen identified as another reason of deleveraging the sterility of credit and the refinancing incapability of corporations. Speculative and credit-driven prosperity may continue for a time, due to, as Veblen (1904, p. 196) noted, the "habit of buoyancy or speculative recklessness". Deflation comes about when speculative prosperity ends. In a general sense, as long as credit-inflation and capitalisation rise, nominal incomes and aggregate demand increase, but real wage and consumption lag behind. Veblen proclaimed that nominal wages eventually begin to rise near the end of prosperity. Rising labour cost decreases the actual and expected earning-capacities. As a result, the solvency risk increases and interruptions in investment spending might come about. Veblen (1923) claimed that the increased earning-capacity during a period of inflated recapitalisation depends on the growth of the price-level for the sales from which the earnings are drawn, or on a decline of production cost. But, the cumulative advance of price-level involves successful freedom from imprudent competition in the market. This can be achieved by collusion and concentration of power in business traffic. However, if solvency ultimately collapses, a liquidity crisis makes the crash inevitable. The crash depends upon the number of corporations and banks that fail to fulfil financial commitments thereby prompting distress and default for other units. As defaults spread, the economy falls into liquidation and debt-deflation processes and financial fragility turns into financial instability. Veblen (1904) maintained that in the period of liquidation the earnings represented by higher leverage go to the creditors outside the industrial process, except if bad debts are written off. The liquidation process, as well as the transfer of ownership to the creditors, depends on the magnitude of contraction in the money value of collateral, the extension of defaults, the rate of interest, solvency risk and effective demand.

In this setting, over-leverage and deleverage are financial processes that institutionalise the cultural adaptation of the macro-system to business values and principles and to pecuniary habits and routines. This adaptation evolves through processes of euphoria, booms, speculative crashes, financial fragility and instability and debt-deflation. Over-leverage, and especially speculative leverage, decidedly depends on the evolving pecuniary financial innovations and institutions and the growth of financial markets. Over-leverage is a habitual process that in due course stimulates inflation and business activity, but, ultimately, causes insolvency and deleverage. Deleverage increases pressures for liquidation of inherited real and financial assets, generating deflation and depression. In Veblen's (1905, p. 462) words,

> movements of general credit and general prices have apparently a mutual accelerating effect upon one another, both in case of advance and in case of decline, giving rise to the well-known cumulative process of expansion or of contraction that marks a period of prosperity or of crisis or depression.

Prosperity spreads because of expectations of higher prices and demand. The higher the leverage, the higher the rise in prices and demand. But eventually, as wages increase, the discrepancy between realised and expected earnings increases, thus resulting in a discrepancy between actual and expected capitalisation. If the banking system denies further liquidity, the value of collateral falls triggering liquidation. Liquidation, in turns, brings a further fall in prices, profits and liquidity flows. Under these circumstances, financial and macroeconomic stability could be restored only through a strong readjustment of values. In the absence of such a readjustment a crisis will eventuate. A crisis is a period of debt-deflation, liquidation, and collapse of capitalisation. In Veblen's system, prosperity at all times leads to depression. However, the latter is not certain that will bring about the required conditions for prosperity. Veblen observed that liquidation corrects over-leverage and overcapitalisation, but prosperity requires expansionary mechanisms of income and liquidity creation. In a period of brisk times, some branches might see their liabilities to become, to some degree, bad debts. In such instances, these branches may be forced by the state of affairs to deliver output at prices that generate profits below what is required to maintain their solvency. In cases like this, the likelihood these branch to default upsurges and hence debt-depression tendencies would ultimately prevail.

Industrial structure, financial structure and macroeconomic change

VFIH illuminates the endogenous instability and the systemic inadequacies of the business enterprise system. In addition, it exposes that the capitalist economies cause insecurity, income inequalities and speculative financial practices that induce waste and economic fluctuations. Nevertheless, one of Veblen's most inspiring observations is that the order and stability of the macro-system depend on the cultural coherence or incoherence among the various sub-systems in the complex and evolving economic and social structure. For Veblen, the main reason why the macro-system behaves in different ways at different times is that the evolving pecuniary financial institutions cause a cultural incoherence between the financial, business and industrial structures. Moreover, VFIH elucidates that pecuniary funding and financing practices in business and banking trigger cumulative erosion of productive activities. A parasitic restructure of capital, which is embodied in business and financial contracts that in turn reflect pecuniary habits and business principles, causes macroeconomic disorder and instability. Veblen's evolutionary theory of macroeconomic change presumes a cultural co-evolution between productive and pecuniary structures that evolves through real historical time. On these grounds, Veblen paid attention to the institutional structure of capital and the pecuniary habits and routines, which, given the state of the industrial arts, stimulate or retard economic growth.

In the context of VFIH, macroeconomic order and stability rely on financial order and stability, which necessitate the efficient allocation of liquidity flows to industry. On the other hand, financial stability hinges on macroeconomic stability and order, which assume an economy in which the productive capacity is capable of creating sustainable income flows to maintain full-employment effective demand. In Veblen's system, the latter is defined as the level of private aggregate demand necessary to absorb the total serviceable output produced. The sustainability of effective demand is decisive because maintainable income flows are a prerequisite for corporations to continuously achieve normal profits so as to preserve their solvency and creditworthiness. Moreover, solvency is a qualification for a corporation to effectively refinance its position-making, to successfully fulfil debt obligations and to actualise investment plans.

Therefore, VFIH contextualises the cultural interconnectedness between financial and macroeconomic order and stability, which are demonstrated by the efficient coordination between income flows resulting from production and distribution processes; and liquidity flows resulting from new borrowing, recapitalisation and refinancing. For Veblen, the effectiveness of this coordination is appraised by the magnitude of waste that characterises every capitalist economy. His perception of waste, indeed, affirms the ramifications of the evolving financial institutions on aggregate demand and, through it, on economic growth and the sustainability of income and liquidity flows. His remarkable statement is that the quality of the financial structure of aggregate demand is the cause and effect of the cultural adaptability of the financial and macro-economic sub-systems to business values and principles.

Veblen focused on two key ways in which the evolving financial institutions damage the quality of the financial structure of aggregate demand. As argued, the first refers to the misallocation of liquidity among corporations and industrial branches. The second refers to the insufficiency of investment in tangible assets. When pecuniary habits dominate corporations' practices, liquidity might be speculatively used to increase the market value of good-will and business capital. Veblen maintained that the purchasing of tangible assets is forward-looking and fluctuates according to variations in investor's confidence about actual and expected profits. If actual profits, made by industrial production and, as I will argue in the next chapter, distribution processes, exceed pecuniary profits businessmen expect to make from positions in financial markets, then investment in tangible assets possibly will increase. However, in the cultural context of VFIH this is not probable.

What is more likely is the cumulative growth of business capital, which is associated with unsustainable leverage processes, manipulation, speculation and parasitic financial practices. Nonetheless, profits and cash flows available to preserve the quality of liability structures and validate past debts depend on the pace of investment in tangible assets. VFIH presumes that there is a cumulative decline in the price of serviceable goods and in tangible and intangible assets, which adversely affect pecuniary profits, recapitalisation and investment. For Veblen, the business traffic is such that actual production persistently diverges from potential serviceable production and output, given the state of the industrial arts. These endogenous divergences between actual and potential output evidence economic fluctuations as a significant systemic feature of capitalist economies. In this sense, Veblen perceived not only economic growth but also business cycles to have a cultural and pecuniary character.

Consequently, in Veblen's macroeconomics, pecuniary debt is destabilising because it increases waste and insufficient demand for serviceable goods. The effect of the evolving financial institutions on private aggregate demand leads to a level of spending that cannot promote high productive employment and community's standard of living. Besides, low demand for serviceable goods reduces actual profits and hence the capacity of debt-holders to meet financial commitments. The cumulative effect of higher levels of parasitic liquidity is, therefore, expected to stimulate fragile and unsustainable leverage structures for firms, households and banks. Veblen was aware of these financial macro-effects as well as of the incapacity of the business enterprise system to maintain long-term parasitic lines of financial manoeuvres and business practices. In his view, there is a constant interface between the macro-system and the habitual frames of mind of those engaged in spending and financing decisions. Macroeconomic evolution is the result of a cumulative process of natural selection of the fittest habits of thought. The direction of this process is uncertain and depends on the degree that industrial capital is being subordinated to its business and pecuniary structure. In other words, the quantitative record of the macro-system builds upon the type of the symbiosis between the industrial and financial systems. In biological terms, the symbiosis can be mutualistic or parasitic. A mutualistic symbiosis occurs when both systems benefit. A parasitic symbiosis occurs when one system (the parasite) benefits and the other system is harmed. Financial innovations and institutions induce selection processes of pecuniary habits of thought and routines, which, in Veblen's cultural, holistic macro-vision, engender a parasitic symbiosis. In this sense, the evolving financial markets and institutions advance the cultural authority of business principles on the macro-system. The consequence is the continuous and cumulative cultivation of systemic, endogenous forces that predispose the macroeconomic behaviour of a credit-driven economy to instability, debt-deflation and depression.

In this cultural setting, Veblen proclaimed that the growth of pecuniary institutions dichotomises the interests of those who exercise the discretion in banking and business from the interests of the community. The major concern of the elite of business and finance is the stability of their pecuniary wealth and not the promotion of employment, growth and community's welfare. As Veblen (1919, p. 93) wrote "the common good, so far as it is a question of material welfare, is evidently best served by an unhampered working of the industrial system at its full capacity, without interruption or dislocation". The financialisation of the business enterprise system fashions certain conditions that cultivate speculative bubbles and financial fragility and institutionalises pecuniary values and principles that, ultimately, undermine a workmanship-led regime of financial stability, full employment and robust economic growth.

Conclusions

In his preoccupation with the real world of economic affairs as well as with economic theory, Veblen found it necessary to disconnect himself from the pre-Darwinian, non-evolutionary method and scope of conventional economics. In the process of estrangement, Veblen envisioned a cultural, holistic theory of macroeconomics. This theory accentuates that in order to understand changes in the structure and functioning of the macro-system, it is vital to relate it to the other parts that constitute the institutional reality of the business enterprise system. He sought to uncover how the prevailing pecuniary cultural scheme of things changed the industrial-productive habitual frame of mind. His primary contention was that since then, productive norms and community's welfare were no longer self-evident to the common sense of finance-driven capitalism.

In his system, cultural evolution brought to the fore the role of pecuniary institutions and values in business and banking decision-making processes in various domains, i.e. allocation of credit, banks' lending practices, the financing of intangible assets and conspicuous consumption, manipulation of asset price, goods price, fraud, etc. The escalation of pecuniary institutions and principles routinises predatory and fraudulent practices that encourage speculation, over-leverage and bubbles, which activate endogenous processes that reduce the quality of organisations' leverage and liability structures and increase financial fragility. In addition, the evolving financial institutions generate liquidity allocation and income distribution inefficiencies that increase parasitic spending and waste. This then causes insufficient demand for serviceable output and discrepancies between actual and potential growth rates.

Veblen developed a macro-vision on the foundations of a cultural theory of capital and effective demand and of a cultural analysis of financial instability. This macro-vision elucidates the unsustainability of pecuniary debt-driven business processes and the validation problems of businessmen and bankers which emanate from parasitic liquidity, consumption and investment activities. In this fashion, the allocation of liquidity and the distribution of income are hypothesised to be predisposed to the disruptive pressures of the evolving financial institutions. Speculative over-leverage, insolvency, deleverage, financial instability, debt-deflation, business cycles and depression emerge as path-dependent developments and endogenous limitations of finance-driven capitalist economies.

Veblen's enduring contribution consists of adding a cultural theory of pecuniary efficiency and waste to the macroeconomic analysis of finance capitalism. This contribution qualifies us to comprehend the institutional origins of industrial inefficiency and decay, as well as to detect the repercussions of financialisation in modern capitalist economies. In Veblen's system of thought, financialisation is a long-term cultural transformation process that establishes the supremacy of pecuniary values and institutions in various realms of decision-making. Besides, Veblen's contribution furnishes us with an insight into the dynamics of the relation between the evolution of financial institutions and the vested interests of the elite of business and finance. Financialisation parasitises an economy's financial and industrial structures. It increases waste, income inequality and financial fragility and establishes debt-deflation, depression and stagnation tendencies. Veblen was unable, within his cultural environment in the early twentieth century, to claim that his cultural, macroeconomic theory could explain major financial and economic catastrophes, like the ones in the 1930s and the 2000s. But for us it is comprehensible to acknowledge that Veblen's theory certainly puts into the epicentre the insights and forces that indeed explain the pragmatic basis of these two Great Crises and recontextualise the foundations of macroeconomics.

Notes

1 It is certainly true that Veblen's cultural, holistic macroeconomic theory does not appear in any of his particular work in a complete form. It must be extracted from many of his writings and especially from his *Theory of the Leisure Class* (1899), *The Theory of Business Enterprise* (1904), *The Instinct of Workmanship and the State of the Industrial Arts* (1914), *The Vested Interests and the Common Man* (1919) and the *Absentee Ownership and Business Enterprise in Recent Times* (1923).

2 Since numerous articles and books of Veblen's thought have been published (see e.g. Anderson, 1933; Dorfman, 1934; Hobson, 1936; Daugert, 1950; Dowd, 1958; Gruchy, 1967; Mitchell, 1969; Hamilton, 1974; Edgell, 1975; Hodgson, 1988; 1992; 2004a; 2004b; Tilman, 1996; Brown, 1998; Louca and Perlman, 2000; Knoedler et al., 2007; Lawson, 2015) there is no need to recount his scientific, methodological and philosophical concepts and contributions here, where attention is almost exclusively paid to his financial macroeconomic ideas.

3 Veblen disputed, as Gruchy (1967) and Hamilton (1974) have analysed, the inherited misleading and incorrect preconceptions of the pre-Darwinian economic thought that prevailed in his time and continue to influence modern mainstream economic theory. Among them, perhaps the most crucial for macroeconomics, is the classical preconceptions of human behaviour and the role of the institutions of money and finance. Regarding human behaviour, it is worth noting Gruchy's (1987) comment that Veblen's concept of the cultural man, or homo culturalis contrasts the concept of the rational man, or, the well-known homo economicus, which structures the micro-foundations of neoclassical economics. According to Gruchy (1987, p. 3), "the individual as homo culturalis is one whose conduct, while reflecting the use of some reason, is nevertheless largely determined by the culture in which individual is placed". Moreover, Ayres (1958) argued that the anthropological conception of culture enabled Veblen to classify classical political economy as pre-Darwinian, because it takes into account that human nature is unaltered. From the viewpoint of Darwinian evolution, all human proclivities, propensities, and wants are formed through a culturally developmental process.

4 Despite the fact that in Veblen's epoch finance and financial markets had not yet gone through the development of the late twentieth century, he envisioned their substantial role in macroeconomic evolution. This fact allowed Veblen, as e.g. Raines and Leathers (1992; 1993; 2000; 2008), Medlen (2003), Dimand (2004), Cornehls (2004), Atkinson (2007) and Argitis (2013a; 2016) recognised, to be one of the first major economists who declared the decisive role of finance and of the evolution of financial institutions.

5 See Veblen (1898; 1899a; 1899b; 1899c; 1900; 1906; 1908a; 1909).

6 Dente (1977, p. 7), was influenced by Zinke (1958), pointed out that "Veblen's institutionalism is a macro-institutionalism". The Veblenian tradition customary underlines the disciplinary effect that technological progress has on the evolution of culture and on habits of thought that determine social order and change. I use the term 'financial macro-institutional mutationism' to focus attention on the significance of financial institutions for macroeconomic order and change.

7 Raines and Leathers (1992, p. 436) argued that in *The Theory of Business Enterprise*, Veblen identified and discussed two major financial product innovations, "the old fashioned loan" and the "stock share". As modern examples they refer stock option futures, interest rate swaps, etc. See also Lawson and Lawson (1990).

8 One can extend this argument to include households so as to generalise Veblen's view in a modern financial macroeconomic context.

9 Veblen (1904, p. 95) noted that "the businessman is under a constant incentive to increase his liabilities and to discount his bills receivable. Indebtedness in this way comes to serve much the same purpose, as regards the rate of earnings, as does a

time-saving improvement in the processes of industry. The effect of the use of credit on the part of a business man so placed is much the same as if his capital had been turned over a greater number of times in the year. It is accordingly to his interests to extend his credit as far as his standing and the state of the market will admit".

10 Gruchy (1967, p. 82) notified that, for Veblen, absentee ownership is "a claim to unearned or free income". Besides, the absentee owner is "an individual who gets something from nothing".

11 For Veblen (1904, pp. 139–140) the good-will "taken in its wider meaning, comprises such things as established customary business relations, reputation for upright dealing, franchises and privileges, trademarks, brands, patent rights, copyrights, exclusive use of special processes guarded by law or by secrecy, and exclusive control of particular sources of materials".

12 Veblen's two methods of rating the value of collateral bears similarities with Minsky's 'two price systems' that establishes his own 'financial instability hypothesis'. It is remarkable that, to my knowledge, Minsky never referred to Veblen's two methods of rating the solvency of corporations.

13 Veblen (1904, p. 154) noted that "the forecast in the case may be more or less sagacious, but, however sagacious, it retains the character of a forecast based on other grounds besides the computation of past results".

14 It is worthy to note that Bolbol and Lovewell (2001) claimed that Veblen's concept of imperfect information and knowledge foreshadowed the insights used by New Keynesian macroeconomics to explain capital market inefficiency.

15 Raines and Leathers (1996; 2000) argued that this is the reason why Veblen's analysis of the functioning of stock markets substantially differs from the efficient financial market hypothesis, and, at the same time, it is very similar to Keynes' conceptualisation of speculative stock markets.

16 Mitchell (1969, p. 628) pinpointed that for Veblen, "the economist is not justified in taking for granted even that the interests of the people who run the enterprise are identical with the enterprise itself".

2 The pragmatic basis of Veblen's approach to economic policy

Introduction

In the previous chapter, I argued that, for Veblen, the order, stability and change of the macro-system are governed by the evolution and transformation of capital. Business principles, pecuniary habits of thought, parasitic financial practices and the vested interests of the elite of business and finance induce: a misallocation of liquidity and a distribution inefficiency, which encourage conspicuous consumption and investment in intangible business capital; low quality asset and liability structures; solvency risk and financial fragility and instability; and higher waste and lower effective demand for serviceable output that permanently reduce actual output below the potential output.

Veblen was mostly concerned about the harmful effects of the aforementioned processes on society's welfare. For him, the financialisation of a capitalist economy, that is the growth of pecuniary habits, values and interests, activates forces that demoralise social prosperity and cohesion. Veblen sadly admitted that in capitalism prosperity turns out to be prosperity of the elite of business and finance. He proclaimed that financial crisis and depression are phenomena that arise from the adaptation of the industrial sector to the evolving financial institutions. He also observed that, as the integration of business and banking sectors becomes more complex, financial fragility and instability and debt-deflation would be more frequent, causing damaging effects on society's security and welfare.

Throughout his writings, Veblen's conception of macroeconomic order, stability and change establishes the pragmatic base of his political economy of reforms and interventions. A noteworthy point to make is that this argument does not automatically denote Veblen's systematic attempt to propose a certain program of institutional and policy reforms. Veblen, indeed, did not propose a complete program of interventions. A possible explanation of this might be associated with the historical period in which Veblen developed his macro-policy thinking. In his time, macroeconomic management was immature and in the shadow of the conceptions of that era concerning the automatic and self-equilibrating forces of the national and international markets. In addition, Veblen never experienced the economic policies of the American New Deal, and, of course, he lacked the knowledge of many discussions around economic policy that took place later. Another possible reason, and perhaps the most significant one, is that Veblen was unwilling to give much prominence to government institutions and policy-makers than he did to their cultural environment. This is reasonable because, as Plotkin and Tilman (2011, p. 7) point out, "Veblen did not want to make exploitation easier, nor did he want to help predatory institutions work any better than they already do". In numerous passages, as noted below, Veblen's conceptualisation of economic policy blends scepticism and pessimism with valuable institutional and policy guidelines that can bring about potentials for a more stable and efficient capitalist order. In any case, his practical economic policy ideas and position may be characterised as an attack to laissez-faire and to private property, and, above all, to parasitic, finance capitalism.

The pessimistic policy bias of Veblen's macro-sociology

Veblen's macroeconomic theory contextualises economic policy as a cultural process that continuously adapts to the evolving financial institutions and the vested interests of the elite of business and banking. Veblen's macro-sociology contextualises his thinking about the social and anthropological foundations of this adaptation process, which discloses the institutional channels through which the prevailing instincts and habits of mind authorise pecuniary efficiency and demoralise industrial and macroeconomic efficiency. In addition, these institutional channels expose the business enterprise system's lack of sustainability constituting it economically unviable to maintain a social order.

More specifically, Veblen's macro-sociology introduces psychological and anthropological 'fundamentals' into his cultural, holistic theory of economic and social change. These 'fundamentals' tolerate the formulation of a political economy vision that puts emphasis on the repercussions that arise from, as O'Hara (1993; 2000) pointed out, the antithesis between positive and negative instincts in human behaviour, principally between the instinct of workmanship and the predatory and emulative instincts. This particular antithesis of instincts leads to Veblen's functional dichotomy of capital between industrial and business capital. Yet, this dichotomy frames Veblen's habits of mind when he envisioned his evolutionary theory of macroeconomic change. In this regard, Edgell (1975, pp. 270–271) pinpointed that Veblen "consistently investigated particular phenomena such as production, consumption and competition, and developed theories related to them, always in the context of his general evolutionary theory". Indeed, for Veblen (1914; 1919), the promotion of industrial capital and of income creation processes depends upon the institutional supremacy of the instinct of workmanship. In his macro-vision, this is a fundamental prerequisite for advancing industrial efficiency and minimising waste. But, as Veblen (1919) maintained, the institutionalisation of the instinct of workmanship depends upon the prior institutionalisation of the material interests and the norms of thought of workers and engineers in public policy.

This insight fashions crucial political economy implications. The launch of the 'politics of workmanship', or what alternatively could be entitled as the 'politics of full employment', in economic policy-making is vital for prompting technological change, productivity and economic growth. Dente (1977, p. 193) noted that Veblen ascribes the abovementioned positive effects of workmanship to parental bent. The latter "is a pattern of social responsibility that makes the instinct of workmanship serviceable for the ends of the community". However, the instinct of workmanship discredits the business trait of self-interest. Moreover, the institutionalisation of the instinct of workmanship motivates economic processes and social dynamics that impede the financialisation of the business enterprise system and, more notably, devitalise the vested interests of the elite of business and finance. Workmanship obliges norms of thought and routines that motivate people to join in productive activities, which increase economic surplus and, under certain conditions, society's prosperity. What is even more interesting is that Veblen envisioned the institutionalisation of the instinct of workmanship as an indispensable precondition for lowering inequality in the distribution of income.

Gruchy (1958, p. 169) argued that in Veblen's system, the ascendancy of the discipline of workmanship depends on the following three arrangements; first, on the elimination of the institution of private property. Common ownership is the manner of an institutional reform which reassures that the entire economic surplus could be used as input to industrial system for the further production of serviceable output. Second, on the capability of the social group of technicians, scientists and engineers to head a national economic planning council; and third, on the design of a national economic budget that would efficiently allocate resources and coordinate economic activities, so as to equalise investment and saving. In other words, the institutionalisation of the instinct of workmanship is the foundation stone for building a mutual relation between financial and industrial systems and for improving efficiency in liquidity allocation. In the same line of argument, Dente (1977, p. 183) underlined that the instinct of workmanship is an essential element of Veblen's political support for the social role of a technical elite who is capable of maximising community's welfare. For Veblen, the efficiency experts (principally engineers and workers) could play a key role in economic policy decision-making by exercising power supportive of high and sustainable growth rates of serviceable goods.

In contrast, the institutionalisation of predation and emulation instincts results in pecuniary habits of mind and institutions (Edgell, 1975). Veblen's macroeconomics indeed encapsulates the repercussions of the prevailing predatory instincts and pecuniary habits of cultural evolution. Business activities and financial contracts and relations routinise predatory instincts and devitalise the instinct of workmanship. In this context, manipulation, speculation and fraud institutionalise the more predatory instincts and practices. The launch of the 'politics of predatory and emulative instincts' in economic policy-making encourages financial processes and triggers dynamics that are vital for serving the vested interests of the elite of business and finance. This elite seeks to succeed in emulation by escalating private property, absentee ownership and parasitic profit-making positions. Gruchy (1967, p. 114) remarked that

> ownership of pecuniary assets frequently acts as a barrier to the full expression of the workmanship drive and to the free functioning of the

industrial system. Instead of being a productive factor entitled to remuneration, ownership, in Veblen's analysis, is a totally unproductive factor.

Veblen (1923) upheld that industry promotes workmanship and business promotes the capitalised value of presumptive earnings. In the context of VFIH (Veblen's 'financial instability hypothesis'), as was commented before, the growth of unproductive profit-making positions eventually brings about insolvent balance sheets and sets limits to the growth of business capital. In addition, the growth of parasitic business practices and activities causes distribution effects that, as argued below in detail, increase waste and reduce the effective demand for serviceable goods. Seen from another angle, the financialisation of the business enterprise system encourages predatory routines and practices that delink finance from the machine processes inducing macroeconomic disorder.

Therefore, for Veblen, the growth of, especially unregulated, corporations, banks and financial markets aggravates, as Hall et al. (2012) pointed out, the habitualisation of predatory instincts and routines. Veblen emphasised that these predatory institutions primarily serve the invidious interests of the ruling classes. The relation of these classes to the economic process is, as Veblen (1899c) stated in his *Theory of Leisure Class*, a relation to acquisition and exploitation and not one of production and serviceability. This viewpoint relies on Veblen's analysis of the desirable social status of individuals in the predatory and barbaric stages of social evolution. Veblen asserted that the evaluation of social status was based on individual's will to be disserviceable to the community. Furthermore, Veblen highlighted that emulation was the instinct that drove men to grapple for reputation and social distinction. Similarly in capitalism, the elite of business and finance establish institutions that disconnect their status and material interests from production and community's serviceability. These institutions cause allocation and distribution inefficiencies that destroy social welfare and impede economic growth.

In this way, Veblen's financial macro-sociology brings to light the importance of predatory and emulation instincts in macroeconomic behaviour. These instincts motivate certain habits of thought and routines in business and banking, which induce parasitic financing processes, speculative bubbles and low quality leverage and liability structures. At the micro-level, predatory and fraudulent practices determine the distribution of surplus product and liquidity among the 'captains of business and finance'. At the macro-level, as Argitis (2016, p. 848) argued, "profits and cash flows depend on the risk that the financial structure of effective demand carries on due to predatory practices in financial markets". Above and beyond, Veblen's financial macro-sociology discloses the anthropological presuppositions of policy interventions. Throughout his writings, Veblen seemed to endorse that economic policy-making adapts itself to the predominant instincts, habits, routines and institutions. This occurs because policy-makers participate into learning processes that adapt their mentality and frame of mind to pecuniary habits of thought that legitimise business values and principles. In this manner, Veblen's financial macro-sociology inaugurates a pessimistic bias into his political economy concerning the subject of the feasibility of economic policy to change the sequence of affairs. Too often in his writings, Veblen appeared to believe that, given the pecuniary nature of institutional setting, economic theory and political ideologies ultimately offer the functional intellectuality to predatory classes to augment their power over institutions and the interest of the common man.

Income distribution, effective demand and economic growth

Despite the pessimistic policy bias of Veblen's financial macro-sociology, there are indications, throughout his writings, that he envisioned institutional reforms and policy interventions that aim at creating possibilities for improving community's welfare. At a macro-level, Veblen seemed to think about the means to push actual growth rate as close as to potential growth rate, and the employment close to full employment. In this regard, he placed emphasis on the state of the industrial arts that positively affect industrial efficiency; the allocation efficiency of liquidity, which keeps industrial branches in order and eliminates the likelihood of financial instability; and the distribution efficiency, which reduces inequality and waste and stimulates effective demand for serviceable goods. Arguably, these factors could be seen as the fundamental pillars of Veblen's social program of reforms. It is worth noting in advance that the manifestation of such a program presumes the supremacy of the instinct of workmanship. Furthermore, the abovementioned three pillars reveal Veblen's brilliant disposition of the interdependence of the supply- and demand-side of an economy.

The supply-side is exposed by the state of the industrial arts, which lays emphasis on the importance of technological knowledge and popular education. Veblen (1919, p. 56) remarked that the state of the industrial arts "is the indispensable conditioning circumstance which determines the productive capacity of any given community. And this is true in a peculiar degree under this new order of industry, in which the industrial arts have reached an unexampled development". In the following passage, Veblen (1919, p. 56) defined the state of the industrial arts as "the community's joint stock of technological knowledge", and he proclaimed that it determines the technical conditions of production, as well as the maximum production that a society is capable of achieving, given workers' productivity. In Veblen's (1919, p. 55) words,

> the possible or potential productive capacity of any given community, having the disposal of a given complement of man power and material resources, is a matter of the state of the industrial arts, the technological knowledge, which the community has the use of. This sets the limit, determines the 'maximum' production of which the community is capable.

Regarding the actual level of production, Veblen (1919, p. 55) argued that it is

> determined by the extent to which the available technological efficiency in turned to account; which is regulated in part by the intelligence, or 'education', of the working population, and in greater part by market

conditions which decide how large a product it will be profitable for the business men to turn out.

Dente (1977) pinpointed that, for Veblen, the divergence between actual and potential growth rates is crucial. The reason is that this divergence validates why the concept of economic growth is not synonymous with the concept of community's welfare. Veblen endorsed that the potential serviceable output is always greater than the actual output in the business enterprise system, so there is a welfare gap. Veblen explained this gap as a repercussion of absentee ownership and pecuniary efficiency. However, the antithesis between industrial and pecuniary efficiency enabled Veblen to focus attention on the demand-side and the absorption problem of the serviceable output produced.

Veblen's supply-side analysis of economic growth is modified when he introduced pecuniary debt into his macroeconomic system. In a credit economy, the state of the industrial arts and technological change mostly depend on the financing and funding practices in business and banking. The incorporation of debt and liability structures allowed Veblen to visualise, on the one hand, the composition of the output produced and, on the other hand, the actual use of the surplus product or net industrial product.[1] Veblen considered the size of the surplus product used as input in industrial production as a fundamental growth principle. Gruchy (1958) and Dente (1977) argued that for Veblen, the ideal precondition for maximum economic growth is that the entire surplus product must be industrially serviceable input, so that output will sustainably increase in the future. However, this is impossible to happen in the business enterprise system, because, as Veblen maintained, the prevailing habits of thought demote industrial efficiency and establish the price systems of goods and assets as key institutional coordinator of pecuniary efficiency. But, if industrial efficiency is sacrificed for pecuniary efficiency, the actual growth rate is, 'naturally', less than the potential growth rate. Veblen used the institution of the price system to contemplate the high interdependence between aggregate supply of serviceable goods and effective demand.

As already commented, in Veblen's system, effective demand is the aggregate spending that determines industry's capacity of converting saleable serviceable goods into money values. Veblen hypothesised that in the business enterprise system there is a continuous problem of insufficient private demand due to the pecuniary nature of consumption and investment. He upheld that private expenditures cannot sustain effective demand at the full employment level because of the parasitic and wasteful use of surplus product. What is crucial in Veblen's argument is the idea that the pecuniary private aggregate spending is susceptible to the prevailing habits and routines that frame the mind and behaviour of consumers and investors. Along these lines, Veblen understood and endorsed the cultural and pecuniary character of the phenomena of 'over-production' and 'under-consumption'. He proclaimed that the profit realisation problems of corporations depict the circumstance that there is not effective demand close to industry's full capacity. According to Veblen (1919, pp. 63–64) there is constant danger of over-production. So that there is commonly a large volume of man power unemployed and an appreciable proportion of the industrial plant lying idle or half idle. It is quite unusual, perhaps altogether out of the question, to let all or nearly all the available plant and man power run at full capacity even for a limited time.

Therefore, Veblen was well aware of a capitalist economy's permanent divergence from full employment output, which comes about because of parasitic practices that increase waste and reduce effective demand. This conception contextualises, what can, arguably, be stated as, Veblen's 'cultural and institutional aspects of full employment'. Involuntary unemployment emerges as the macroeconomic cost of abandoning the discipline of workmanship and industrial efficiency. In other words, involuntary unemployment exists because a large share of the economic surplus goes to vested interests and is spent on conspicuous consumption and investment in intangible assets.

Dente (1977) claimed that Veblen was indeed concerned with the problem of distribution inefficiency. In Veblen's system, income inequality is crucial not only for distributive justice, but also for industrial inefficiency. It is hypothesised that there is an inverse relation between distribution inefficiency and industrial efficiency. The higher income inequality, the higher the share of the economic surplus that goes to vested interests and to parasitic spending. For Veblen, income inequality is evidence of pecuniary efficiency and low growth rates or stagnation. As was argued in the previous chapter, in the context of VFIH, decisions to invest in tangible or intangible assets are taken conditionally to the expected actual and pecuniary profits. Expected profits depend on variations in the price systems of goods and assets as well as on the financing environment. The structure and quality of organisations' balance sheets reflect the mix of internal and external funds used in prior investment in tangible and intangible assets. The sustainability of the expected income and cash flows relies on the volume of investment in tangible assets and on effective demand. On the other hand, the growth of pecuniary institutions and distribution inefficiency decrease both the internal and external cash flows. Uncertainty over cash flows and solvency risk increases due to misallocation of liquidity and distribution inefficiency, which divert the economic surplus from its purpose as input for the production of serviceable goods. This effect cumulatively damages the growth potentials.

Therefore, distribution inefficiency increases organisations' solvency risk. As was argued, tangible assets are the assets that represent the earning-capacity of corporation's productive property; whereas intangible assets represent pecuniary profits and capital gains that cannot be attributed to productive sources. Veblen (1919, p. 70) proclaimed that pecuniary profit

represents no contribution to the output of goods and services, but only an effectual claim to a share in the annual dividend, on grounds which appear to be legally honest, but which cannot be stated in terms of mechanical cause and effect, or of productive efficiency.

In this regard, Veblen emphasised that the income claimed by intangible assets emanates from financial contracts that are immaterial relations, and is drawn from the product surplus. The industrial system is therefore the productive source of the returns on both tangible and intangible assets. Since the income creation source of both is the same, the distribution process raises certain concerns because returns on intangible assets are not a return for the productive use of the plant, but for exercising ownership and control of industry. In other words, they are returns that hinge upon pecuniary efficiency.

Veblen identified that in the new industrial order unconventional methods to increase pecuniary profits are at the epicentre of business concerns. One of the methods used by managers is to sabotage the process of production, so as to purposefully reduce the output produced and augment the difference between the price of goods and the cost of production. As noted before, the sustainability of the market value of a corporation's capitalisation is imperative for the conduct of industrial business in financial markets. Veblen (1919, p. 73) asserted that for the prosperity of business it is very important to maintain the output produced within reasonable limits "to maintain reasonably profitable prices; that is to say, such prices as will yield the largest obtainable net return to the concerns engaged in the business". Veblen connected this largest obtainable net return with the principle of "charging what the traffic will bear". But his most useful observation is that these unconventional practices damage social welfare. In particular, Veblen (1919, p. 76) observed that

> the strategic curtailment of net production below productive capacity is net loss to the community as a whole, including both the business men and their customers; the gains which go to these business concerns in this way are net loss to the community as a whole, exclusive of the business concerns and their investors.

Furthermore, Veblen (1923, p. 10) upheld that the business interests do not match in any passable degree with the interests of the underlying population. "The material interest of the underlying population is best served by a maximum output at a low cost, while the business interests of the industry's owners may best be served by a moderate output at an enhanced price". This conflict of interests stems from the fact that the industrial system is under the control of the elite of business and finance, who are skilled in manipulating prices and not in advancing industrial efficiency and community's welfare. The logic of his argument relies on the fact that pecuniary gains are made by variations in the price systems of goods and assets.

What is even more impressive in Veblen's analysis, as Dente (1977) has underlined, is that the growth of pecuniary institutions was the institutional ground for installing the rate of workmanship within the price system. The rate of workmanship is the price of labour. The cost of labour is part of the production cost. But, businessmen and bankers use the price systems of goods and assets to rate efficiency in terms of pecuniary gain. Accordingly, the rate of workmanship, or in other words the wage rate, is disciplined by pecuniary efficiency as a going concern. Any increase in wages and any effort to increase employment and redistribute income at the expense of vested interests, it would be immediately adversely evaluated by business concerns in terms of pecuniary efficiency. Veblen argued that the discipline of workers and the control of labour-cost is another method used by vested interests to increase pecuniary profits and to maintain the market value of an organisation's capitalisation and good-will. Moreover, he claimed that since the profits of corporations and invested capital are derived from the margin of sales price over-production cost, business managers seek to curtail production cost as much as it is possible. However, reductions of production-cost would be reasonable within the logic of business enterprise, only if they are curtailments of expenditures on those factors of production which, as Veblen (1923, p. 393) argued, "are not capitalised or included among the rateable assets of the business community. Which comes to saying that the curtailment, if any, must take effect in those expenditures which go to the industrial man-power and the outlying farm population".

By noting this business principle, Veblen accentuated his concern about the conflict between the interests of the One Big Union and the interests of workers that are enunciated by trade-unions. Veblen (1923, pp. 394–395) maintained that as organisers of industrial man-power, trade-unions "are consistently endeavouring, with the fluctuating measure of success, to enforce an indefinitely extensible claim in the way of better pay". Nevertheless, he claimed that a better pay for workers is significant for aggregate demand and well-being only if it induces a higher real wage. A better pay is better only in terms of price. The better-paid workers are at the same time consumers of the goods whose prices increase, when credit augments. As a result, Veblen asserted that inflation would erode the real wages.

In Veblen's system, the distribution of income is among the fundamental factors that influence macroeconomic stability, order and change. His conceptualisation revolved around the repercussions of distribution inefficiency. He used the categories of conspicuous consumption and investment in intangible assets as examples of the destabilising effects of a parasitic and unequal income distribution. Given Veblen's preconceptions and habits of mind, these forms of expenditures generate waste and industrial inefficiency. Veblen stated that wages and profits that arise from productive employment and accumulation of tangible capital are customary income sources for expenditures that increase effective demand for serviceable output, and, hence, industrial efficiency and economic growth. For Veblen, workers must increase their consumption. For this to happen, they must first obtain a higher share of national income. Conversely, the leisure class must consume on a smaller scale. Therefore, Veblen rejected the classical view that income inequality drives economic growth. In addition, he pinpointed the role of the evolving habits, routines and social status in influencing the propensity to consume and to save of different social groups and especially of the leisure class. Nevertheless, he admitted that the distribution of economic surplus favours businessmen and bankers. Besides, he underlined the role of emulation as a principle of consumer's irrational behaviour and parasitic spending. Dente (1977, p. 13) noted that for Veblen, "emulation dominates utilitarian consumption activities. This emulation leads to conspicuous consumption based on envy and jealousy". Emulation is a strong motive for men to accumulate wealth, which is evidence of pecuniary efficiency, honour and power. In Veblen's political economy, a more equal distribution of income would restructure private spending in such a way that it would allow the use of a higher share of surplus product as input for further improvement of industrial efficiency. Therefore, a more equal distribution of income is a necessary precondition for a society to reduce waste and to increase the actual and potential growth rates. Furthermore, in the context of VFIH, when the actual growth rate increases, the capacity of organisations to fulfil debt commitments improves. In this context, income inequality increases the likelihood of financial fragility and instability.

Nevertheless, for Veblen, income distribution could be more equal only if the hierarchy of social and political power would promulgate the interest of the efficiency experts and workers, and not the interest of the business and finance experts. The pragmatic basis of his political economy enabled Veblen to realise that the power and authority of making key economic choices about income distribution are in the hands of managers, bankers and businessmen. These social groups undergo business and financial risks and receive unearned incomes far in excess of what they spend to sustain emulation and conspicuous consumption for prestige. Thus, for Veblen, a fundamental principle of economic policy is the reduction of the parasitic share of surplus income that validates wasteful spending; and the increase of the income share of the efficiency experts and workers, which promotes productive spending. But, as Veblen sadly admitted, this distribution principle is unlikely to be institutionalised in a capitalist economy characterised by private property, absentee ownership and the supremacy of business principles.[2] For this reason, he endorsed the need for property arrangements that would enable society to use the economic surplus not for serving the social status and prestige of the leisure class, but as inputs for industrial growth, employment and welfare. Nonetheless, new property arrangements can come about only if the regime of workmanship gains ascendancy. The enhancement of community's welfare is not a harmonious process, but one that comes along with conflicts of habits, values and interests. Social well-being is adequate only when financial institutions encourage technological process, productive employment and industrial efficiency. The growth of pecuniary habits and interests is evidence of lower flows of material goods and services to society.

Fiscal policy and aggregate demand

Despite the fact, as many scholars have observed, that Veblen was not affectionate to capitalism, he discussed and envisioned aggregate demand management policies to cope with the intrinsic problems of over-production or under-consumption.[3] As I have already underlined, Veblen's exposition of the evolution of capital heavily relies on his preconception about the vital differences among a 'natural economy', a 'money economy' and a 'credit economy'. Veblen's theory of business enterprise is a monetary theory of production,[4] where the evolving financial institutions have widened the gap between economy's capacity to produce and capacity to absorb the serviceable output produced. In this regard, Vining (1939) noted that Veblen should be included among the first authors who anticipated Keynes's principle of effective demand. In the same line of argument, Gruchy (1958) notified that for Veblen, a laissez-faire capitalism is unable to resolve by itself the problem of insufficient demand and to reach full employment conditions. What is vital in Veblen's analysis is that he directly connected the problem of insufficient effective demand to the liquidity allocation and income distribution inefficiencies of the business enterprise system, and, above all, to the evolving pecuniary institutions. He hypothesised an inverse relation between the effective demand for serviceable output and the share of economic surplus that goes to vested interests, because a relatively small portion of it goes to private investment in tangible assets and to non-conspicuous consumption.

Veblen delineated four sources of aggregate demand.[5] The first source is private consumption spending. He divided private consumption into "conspicuous, emulative and instrumental consumption" (Mouhammed, 1999, p. 596). Conspicuous consumption principally reflects the predation and parasitism of the leisure class. The concept of conspicuous consumption relies on the motivation to spend money income on the purchasing of non-serviceable, luxury and high-status goods and services whose usage publicly display economic power and wealth. Veblen recognised that to the conspicuous consumer this public display economic power is a means of achieving or preserving a given social power and prestige either real or perceived. In Veblen's macro-system, high levels of conspicuous consumption are undesirable on the ground and that they are an indicator of parasitic income and of high levels of income inequality, waste and industrial inefficiency. Thus, when conspicuous consumption increases, the rate of growth is hypothesised to slow down or decrease because of inadequate consumption of serviceable output.[6]

The concept of emulative consumption is used by Veblen to elucidate that individuals mostly suffer from a continuing dissatisfaction in relation to their consumption patterns (Mouhammed, 1999). In contrast, instrumental consumption satisfies human needs. The hypothesis made by Veblen is that income distribution, and especially the share of economic surplus possessed by the leisure class, affects the allocation of consumption spending between serviceable and non-serviceable goods. The logic behind this hypothesis is that any increase in the share of consumption spending for non-serviceable goods to total consumption spending reduces effective demand, the rate of economic growth and the sustainability of community's welfare.

The second source of aggregate demand emanates from private investment expenditures. VFIH illustrates the cultural and financial setting in which corporations take investment decisions, and, furthermore, interprets investment volatility and the destabilising effect on economic growth. As noted above, Veblen distinguished between actual and pecuniary profits to explain investment in tangible and intangible assets. Industrial investment increases when expected profits from production exceed the cost of a given leverage structure. For so long as this difference exists, businessmen will seek to increase debt to finance the accumulation of tangible assets. Industrial investment expenditures cause a positive effect on productivity, employment and effective demand. Veblen paid particular attention to corporations' profits not only because they are a prime source of internal funds, but also because they are liquidity flows that can be used to fulfil debt commitments. When there is a constant inadequacy of reasonable profits then investment decreases and the solvency and default risks increase. Veblen (1904, p. 255) argued that when such is the case, the remedy is either a higher aggregate demand or the elimination of cutthroat competition that keeps profits below from what businessmen view as reasonable level. Aggregate expenditures, productive and wasteful, bring about higher prices, and hence corporations would be capable of maintaining profits, investments, solvency and capitalisation. In addition, if the increase in demand is sufficiently large, corporations could alleviate pressures on prices caused by sabotage and cutthroat competition. Nevertheless, the key point in Veblen's analysis is that aggregate private demand cannot absorb the surplus product of industry. This enabled Veblen to diagnose the need for a civilised government to get involved in business traffic.

The third source of aggregate demand comes from the government sector. Veblen (1904, p. 256) originally argued that government spending for "armaments, public edifices, courtly and diplomatic establishments, and the like" is almost wasteful. He proclaimed that government expenditures must be appraised conditional to their input to industrial efficiency. In this manner, government spending is a pure waste, because it withdraws resources from the industrial process. However, Veblen recognised that wasteful expenditures may, eventually, increase the effective demand for serviceable goods. Without these expenditures business and industry would decline, followed by depression and instability. Consequently, Veblen concluded that wasteful expenditures bring prosperity and benefits to the community, since they increase the vendibility of the output produced and the utilisation of industrial capacity. Besides, he claimed that government expenditures induce, in due course, a positive effect on industrial efficiency. This then increases aggregate income and community's wealth. It is worthy to note that Veblen remarked that economic growth would be sustainable, only if there were a permanent fiscal stimulus. This insight might reveal that Veblen supported the implementation of an expansionary fiscal policy. He was also concerned about the expansionary impact of wasteful expenditures. He saw government expenditures financed by taxes as less expedient than the expenditures financed by debt. In addition, he underlined the peculiar advantage of higher indirect taxes on the prices of goods and on business profits.

What is even more remarkable is Veblen's (1904, p. 256) insight that government spending has

> the additional advantage that the public securities which represent this waste serve as attractive investment securities for private savings, at the same time that, taken in the aggregate, the savings so invested are purely fictitious savings and therefore do not act to lower profits or prices.

From this passage, it is reasonable to argue that Veblen seemed to acknowledge investors' preference for holding low-risk government securities in their portfolios. In the context of VFIH, the combination of higher government expenditures and low-risk government securities increases corporate profits and the market value of collateral and reduces solvency risk. Veblen (1904, p. 252, footnote 1) indicated that government expenditures

> act unequivocally to advance the values of the business men's holdings and increase their gains, as counted in business terms. The wasteful expenditure is good for trade. It is only in the eventual liquidation that a disadvantageous business consequence comes in view.

Overall, Veblen seemed to visualise government intervention as an institutional and policy change that stabilises the financial and macroeconomic systems and improves social welfare.

Nevertheless, Veblen argued that the sum of private and public expenditures is likely to be insufficient to absorb the surplus product of the machine industry. As a result, the actual growth rate would not increase that much to attain the full employment growth rate. The shortage of expenditures, Veblen asserted, is higher on every occasion that there is significant technological progress and higher income inequality that accumulates savings in relatively few hands. In these circumstances, Veblen examined the importance of a fourth source of aggregate demand. This source springs from foreign countries through imperialism and is an additional factor that could absorb the surplus output. Mouhammed (1999) claimed that Veblen considered foreign demand as a factor that creates and maintains profits for the vested interests of those who are engaged in the making of private gain in foreign investment, foreign concessions and export trade.

In Veblen's macro-framework, given the price-level, the output supply adjusts to the needs of national and international markets that determine the volume of effective demand. Veblen hypothesised that corporations generate profits and increase investment expenditures as long as the market absorbs the output supplied. However, because of the pecuniary nature of the prevailing financial institutions, output and employment are susceptible to an insufficient aggregate demand. As a result, Veblen endorsed institutional arrangements and fiscal policy interventions so as to stabilise the industrial system and advance industrial efficiency. For Gruchy (1958, p. 167), Veblen's most remarkable fiscal ideas are "the transfer of the means of production to public ownership, the setting up of national economic planning council, and the construction of national economic budgets for the coordination and guidance of economic activities". Gruchy laid particular attention to the central economic planning council or, as Veblen calls it, the central industrial directorate, whose objective ought to be the higher industrial production and social welfare. Veblen stressed the important role of the central industrial directorate in the collection of information regarding a nation's productive capacities. This information is essential for any economy to improve the efficient use of the available resources. Furthermore, Gruchy (1958, p. 169) marked out that "the central planning body would construct national economic budgets that would indicate the nation's expanding total production in some future planning period and also the desired distribution of this output among various groups of users". Veblen conceptualised the national economic budget as a supplement to the price system in the allocation of economic resources. He also fully understood the problem of harmony between individual and collective economic preferences that the nation's economic budget has to resolve, as Gruchy (1958, p. 170) pointed out, "in accordance with a system of democratically approved national priorities".

Monetary policy and financial stability

Veblen's analysis of macroeconomic management also incorporates monetary policy and regulatory structures to control the growth of business capital. In his viewpoint, these interventions should be examined in relation to his cultural, holistic macro-theorisation of the business enterprise system. As a result, Veblen considered monetary policy as a cultural, monetary process and the interest rate as a cultural-monetary phenomenon. The first point to stress is that a significant insight of Veblen's monetary analysis is the endogeneity of money supply determination, and the examination of this process in terms of credit-driven industrial and pecuniary processes of asset and liability creation. VFIH demonstrates that credit demand is principally determined by speculative processes of over-leverage, recapitalisation and business expansion. In addition, credit demand results from corporations' liquidity needs for financing investment in tangible capital. On the other hand, VFIH illustrates that the capacity of the financial system to expand credit depends upon the prevailing institutions in banking and in business traffic. As argued in the previous chapter, the desire of bankers and their business customers to increase assets and liabilities depends upon evaluations of corporations' solvency risk and capability to meet payments due to debts. Therefore, credit supply relies on anticipations of corporations' solvency risk and expected profits, which, in turn, determine the solvency risk of banks. Note that in Veblen's system, credit supply inefficiencies and constraints have certain implications for understanding income creation and distribution processes that crucially affect both financial and macroeconomic order and change.

A second point to stress is that in Veblen's banking analysis loans exceed reserves. According to Veblen (1904, p. 101) "it is a business truism that no banking house could at a moment meet all its outstanding obligations. A necessary source of banking profits, e.g., is a large excess of the volume of business over reserves". In this monetary framework, Veblen comprehended the interest rate as a factor which is directly involved in the determination of the solvency risk of both corporations and banks. He underlined that the interest rate is a benchmark below which profits must not fall. When corporations build their leverage structures, they agree to fulfil debt commitments. Veblen (1904) claimed that these outstanding obligations may have been negotiated at an earlier period when expected profits were higher. Solvency presumes that the rate of expected earnings must exceed the rate of interest cost to make debt serviceable. However, if interest payments rise significantly, relative to corporation's actual earning-capacity due to an increase in the interest rate, then they will be forced to increase their borrowing to cover their liabilities. This effect may reveal that Veblen endorsed an easy money policy. In addition, it is worth noting that for Veblen it was crucial that monetary policy-makers should not only keep the interest rate low, but also improve the allocation efficiency of liquidity to minimise corporations' solvency and default risks. Above and beyond, one more noteworthy idea advanced by Veblen, as Raines and Leathers (2008) pointed out, is that government sectors should extend credit to certain sections of the business community to preclude financial fragility.

Veblen's analysis of corporation's financial structure and solvency risk draws certain implications for the manipulation of the interest rate by bankers. As argued in the previous chapter, the manipulation of the interest rate misinforms investors about the quality of the liability structures, and, as Raines and Leathers (2008) pinpointed, the capitalised valuation of business assets and bonds. This is crucial for banks' solvency risk as well as for the stability of the wealth of the elite of business and finance. Yet, Veblen was fully aware that a low rate of interest could encourage corporation's investment in intangible assets and allow the accumulation of business capital to proceed unimpeded. Thus, in his viewpoint, the most crucial is the direct impact of monetary policy and of the interest rate on the structure of capital. If investment in tangible capital increases, then the easy money policy will encourage and sustain economic growth. If investment in intangible capital eventually increases, then the easy money policy will boost business capital and make an economy's financial structure susceptible to parasitic spending and speculative bubbles.

Discussing the significance of Veblen's endogenous analysis of credit creation helps to focus on the correlation between capitalisation and speculative credit-inflation. As Veblen used it, credit-inflation progressively increases as a result of the expanded volume of purchasing-power, which arises out of the supply of credit and the creation of over-leveraging structures. Besides, corporations, which experience higher goods and asset price, may increase investment spending, thereby expanding aggregate demand. This outcome would further boost the price-level, and to the extent that labour-cost lags behind the inflation rate, it will increase profits as well as leverage and liability. For Veblen, these circumstances largely stem from an endogenous process of speculative credit-driven inflation. This financial process continues until a general liquidation of credits begins. Veblen (1923) extensively discussed the manner in which credit-inflation ultimately undermines the stability of good-will and destabilises recapitalisation. In his analysis, credit-inflation is a key feature of unsustainable speculative prosperity. The business traffic, sooner or later, will begin to deteriorate because of the increased cost of living. Workers' consumption will fall due to inflation, and labour-cost will progressively increase. In addition, investment in cost-reducing technologies will pressure the price-level downwards. Both effects would undermine the stability of profits. The coming debt-deflation would signal the end of speculative credit-inflation.

Veblen's analysis of credit-inflation and debt-deflation enabled him to make significant political economy observations. In particular, Veblen (1923) considered the social, political and monetary policy consequences of the formulation of the

One Big Union of financial interests. The elite of finance gain from the credit-expansion in pecuniary money values at the expense of community's welfare. But, the elite of finance is also concerned about the effect of inflation on the stability of wealth and on the order and stability of the financial system. Veblen (1923) argued that financial stability is a top priority for those who take part in the business of credit-inflation. For this reason, he maintained that the One Big Union of financial interests is very likely to favour controls over the level of credit supplied so as to sustain both the stability of their wealth and the order of the financial system. In this regard, Raines and Leathers (1992, p. 433) argued that Veblenian financial markets combine "both a tendency toward collusive stability and resurgent periods of financial instability". Instability comes from speculative over-leverage, while stability emanates from decisions taken by the elite of finance to approve collusive structures in order to effectively control output and prices. The purpose of such practices is to improve the quality of corporations' liability structures and of banks' asset structure and to advance the competence of managers and bankers to successfully manipulate the price systems.

Nevertheless, financial innovations and over-leverage might increase speculative competition and emulation in business and banking that, in due course, undermine the stability of financial markets. As Argitis (2013a) argued, Veblenian financial stability presumes comprehensive controls of credit. This takes the form of a collusion of large credit institutions, which increase the capacity of controlling both the endogenous creation and the allocation of credit. Veblen (1923) indicated the large investment banks as the financial institutions with the liquidity capacity to reorder industrial branches and merge large corporations. Raines and Leathers (1993, p. 259) notified that the

> large investment bankers emerged in control of the system of credit creation and allocation. From that position, they effectively controlled corporations which dominated the key industries, and ultimately, through the linkages in both the industrial and business systems, controlled the industrial system at large.[7]

Besides, large investment bankers concentrate such financial power and flows of information so that they can manage many of the processes that govern corporations' recapitalisation and solvency. For this reason, Veblen described investment bankers as the master of corporations' solvency. Veblen (1923, p. 339) argued that

> the Investment Banker has emerged, to serve as a powerful instrumental factor in working out the new alignment of ownership and industrial business, and presently to take his place as one of the essential workday institutions of the business community.

Investment bankers apply consolidation practices and concentrate large shares of common stocks and securities that compose corporations' capitalised good-will.

According to Veblen, these practices generate the material basis of the wealth of the elite of finance. Veblen (1923, p. 396) pointed out that

> the One Big Union of the Major Interests and the network of minor concerns through which the business of credit and capitalisation runs, are engaged on a loosely collusive plan for bringing the industrial man-power to reasonable – that is to say profitable – terms by the punitive use of unemployment.

This is a remarkable passage because it reveals that Veblen anticipated that, in the business enterprise system, unemployment is used as a discipline device by the elite of business and finance to control credit-inflation and to manipulate income distribution and asset values. Veblen asserted that the Federal Reserve System represents and promotes the vested interests of absentee owners and the position and prosperity of the wealthy class. The Federal Reserve's policy is designed to manage asset values so as to ensure solvency and stabilise corporations' good-will and recapitalisation, without much conscious concern for the repercussions of such a management upon industrial structures. In Veblen's (1923, p. 226) words, since the funded power and the control of credit are

> in the hands of the associated banking houses and the Federal Reserve, may be able to govern the course of business to such effect as to safeguard the interests of absentee ownership at large, maintain a steadily rising over-capitalisation of absentee assets and assure an indefinitely continued increase of net gain on investments and credit commitments.

But, either way, Veblen (1923, pp. 178–179, note 5) recognised that the creation of the Federal Reserve System was a positive step in protecting financial systems from the risks of insolvency and instability. He pinpointed its power to use the discount rate and to put into operation regulatory structures that reinforce the stability of pecuniary wealth, as well as of the financial system.

In addition, Veblen contemplated the significant role of the Federal Reserve in supporting the Treasury's management of debt and of the federal government funds. Raines and Leathers (1992, p. 438) observed that, for Veblen, the Federal Reserve can "extend, facilitate, simplify and consolidate the unified control of the country's credit arrangements". However, Veblen's (1923, p. 327) conceptualisation of the inherent instability of the financial system qualified him to claim that an economy's financial relations must be organised on a reasonable plan that "would combine stability with a sufficiently flexible administration of details". This concept, so far as Veblen was concerned, introduced financial regulation to control the growth of business capital as a prerequisite for stability. But, once more, Veblen was pessimistic about the possibility of regulating the financial system. Dirlam (1958, cited by Argitis, 2013a, p. 34) remarked that "Veblen would have been sceptical of any financial reform targeted to deal with financial abuses and the restoration of confidence in financial markets, because he believed the financial abuses were the essence of the business enterprise system". This pessimistic tone is customary in Veblen's writings where he steadily disputed the enduring viability of the pecuniary institutions of capitalism. Given that an economy's financial structure is not entirely amenable to institutional control, Veblen seemed to proclaim that macroeconomic change is, ultimately, not predictable in any precise way.

Institutions, economic policy and community's welfare

As portrayed in the preceding discussion, Veblen's macroeconomic theory and policy are all about the institutions that cause and retard change in economic growth and community's welfare. Veblen paid particular attention to how different conditions of culture and power can alter the structure and functioning of the macro-system and its capacity to principally sustain the production of serviceable goods in order to advance community's welfare. By noting this principle, the purpose of Veblen's ideal political economy was to draw institutional reforms and policy interventions that could improve and ensure society's well-being. In this context, Veblen's program of reforms concerns the building of a mutual symbiosis between productive and financial structures from which people derive their livelihood. As a result, for Veblen, economic policy-making should address the supply-side constraints and the demand-side insufficiencies that generate waste and macroeconomic underperformance.

Veblen examined all the important factors that condition the supply of material goods and services. Among them, he highlighted the state of the industrial arts that bring to the fore the importance of industrial technology and knowledge; and the system of business principles and pecuniary institutions, which have a great power upon the behaviour of banking and the allocation of liquidity. The state of the industrial arts, technology and knowledge influence the size of nation's total output, while the evolving financial institutions affect the structure and sustainability of the output produced. The accumulation of tangible and intangible assets determines the functioning, stability and coherence of the macro-system. Veblen's emphasis was not upon the macroeconomic order that is derived by harmonious technological and financial relationships, but rather upon the macroeconomic disorder that ensues from the repercussions of the evolving financial institutions and the predominant predatory instincts and habits.

One of Veblen's most impressive observations was that the expanding output is co-evolved with a growing incapacity of the private markets and of the price system to distribute this output in an equitable manner over all social groups. This principle enabled him to investigate the demand effects of the unearned income in the system of private property. He upheld that the industrial progress recorded by the industrial arts has not been accompanied by similar progress in the institutions that govern distribution efficiency. This cultural gap elevates the predatory behaviour and the distribution pressure of the elite of business and finance over the economic surplus. As already noted, in the business enterprise system, the price sub-systems of goods and assets fail to allocate resources, liquidity and income in a balanced and efficient manner so as to maintain high levels of aggregate demand and economic activity. This failure becomes more apparent as developments in financial markets cause high leverage and liability structures. Powerful corporations and investment bankers apply restrictions to output and curtailments to employed workers in order to manipulate prices in the goods market and securities market to increase their net profits.

In this cultural setting, Veblen visualised institutional interventions and fiscal and monetary policies that operate upon productive processes and sustainable income flows. As stated previously, Veblen appeared to put forward the idea that the major policy objective should be the economy to attain a close approximation to full employment, thereby advancing society's welfare. Note that this suggestion contradicts the policy preferences of the One Big Union of the Major Interests, which seeks to principally achieve pecuniary profits and larger shares of power, income, ownership and prestige. The instruments used by vested interests are sabotages and price manipulation, fraud, beneficial financing conditions and wage and taxes cuts. But this policy strategy increases pecuniary profits, conspicuous consumption and investment in intangible assets. This then leads to credit-inflation and speculative booms that culminate in financial fragility, crises and debt-deflation. For Veblen, this is the unavoidable economic and social cost from the supremacy of predatory instincts and habits of thought that impair the technological and industrial basis of economic growth and community's welfare.

Arguably, modern neo-liberal policies perfectly fit to Veblen's scepticism and concerns. In his cultural setting, neo-liberal policies legitimise predatory instincts and behaviour, pecuniary gains and the vested interests of the elite of business and finance. Deregulation, privatisation, fiscal austerity, price-stability and asset price-targeting by central banks institutionalise business principles and pecuniary habits of thought. However, for Veblen, such policies are, in due course, associated with parasitic over-leverage, speculative bubbles, manipulation, fraud and insolvency. In Veblen's vision, neo-liberalism authorises in the minds of businessmen and bankers the soundness of predatory practices and fraudulent activities. Moreover, Veblen would perhaps agree that the free-market ideology is dangerous because it ostracises the instinct of workmanship. In his system, the damage of the 'invisible hand' depends on the level of private debt, the share of intangible assets to total capital assets, income inequality and the degree that predatory institutions predominate. Given the financial structure of contemporary economies, where private debt ratios are very high in an environment in which greed, frauds and inequality prevail, Veblen would have claimed that neo-liberal policies indeed induce unsustainable leverage and liability structures, insufficient demand, instability and debt-deflation.

For Veblen, the policy problem is to design a system of institutions that dampens instability and advances society's welfare. He grasped that the inherent instability of monetary production economies is due to pecuniary income flows. In his logic, investment in intangible assets cannot validate business debts. Inadequate investment in tangible assets ultimately undermines the sustainability of profits and solvency, and hence recapitalisation and refinancing. For Veblen (1923, p. 404), the key reason for macroeconomic underperformance is the nature of things in capitalism. He observed that as things go in any democratic community, the governmental agencies are administrated by a business like personnel, principles imbued with the habitual bias of business principles, -the principles of ownership; that is to say, under current conditions, the rights, powers, and immunities of absentee ownership.

Since industry is governed by business ends, population's welfare is suppressed by the endeavours of managers to increase pecuniary efficiency. Similarly the means of livelihood and the amenities of life of workers are rated within the price system in pecuniary terms. The policy problem was therefore the development of a policy strategy that would habitualise the instinct of workmanship. This would contribute to financial stability, sustainable economic growth and community's welfare. However, for Veblen, the possibility that this institutional change occurring is unknown.

Veblen (1923, p. 208) upheld that business principles

> are also in great measure decisive in the larger affairs of life, both for the individual in his civil relations and for the community at large in its political concerns. Modern (civilised) institutions rest, in great part, on business principles.

Most importantly, Veblen (1904, pp. 208–209) proclaimed that due to the prevailing habits of mind that institutionalise the

> business point of view, in terms of profit and loss, the management of the affairs of the community at large falls by common consent into the hands of businessmen and is guided by business considerations. Hence modern politics is business politics, even apart from the sinister application of the phrase to what is invidiously called corrupt politics.

Many of Veblen's most useful political economy observations stem from his refusal to acclaim the pervading bias of business principles in the governing logic of policy concerns. His cultural macro-vision enabled him to contextualise institutional and policy interventions that are not ruled by the pecuniary price systems and efficiency. He saw that policy institutions, and in particular governments and central banks, could play an active role in containing parasitic behaviour and expenditures. Of course, the problem remains in relation to the way in which the institutional apparatus will be disconnected from business principles and pecuniary values and interests. The protection of community's interests needs a program of reforms and interventions that will overcome the institutional constraints of the business enterprise system. Business traffic and decentralised financial markets are institutional devices that promote pecuniary interests through the price systems. Therefore, they undermine the habitualisation of the instinct of workmanship. Industrial order and efficiency, but also financial stability, require investment in tangible assets used in the production of serviceable products. Business and financial market processes, which revolve around pecuniary prices of intangible assets and conspicuous consumption, initiate destabilising forces into the macro-system. In contrast, Veblen suggested institutional changes that would control business capital and increase industrial coordination.

Reforms that improve the allocation efficiency of liquidity are, indeed, an institutional change in the banking system that stabilises and boosts productive economic activity. In this sense, arguably, Veblen would approve central bank's administrative actions and legislation that should attempt to control and guide the productive allocation of liquidity. VFIH clearly illustrates that such an institutional change modifies economy's financial structure in a manner that it could constrain fragility and cyclical instability. Allocation efficiency means that the banking system and the stock market finance investment and positions in tangible capital assets. To the extent that business corporations increase production and generate sustainable profits, they will improve their financial power to reduce solvency risk. Furthermore, central banks must intervene whenever insolvency threatens capitalisation and triggers conditions for debt-deflation processes. Central banks must enlarge their scope and take institutional initiatives to avert the blooming of pecuniary habits, routines and practices in banking. This notion of central bank's responsibility stands in sharp contrast to monetary and financial policies that they customarily follow to stabilise and protect the income and the power of the wealthy class. In this context, for Veblen, economic policy-makers must look beyond fiscal and monetary techniques and instruments. A program of fiscal, monetary and financial reforms can only be effective as a part of a program of institutional reforms that establish the instinct of workmanship. Financial fragility, instability and debt-deflation will recurrently occur as long as policy-makers encourage business investment, conspicuous consumption and absentee ownership.

Concluding, Veblen's work delves deeply into the cultural relationships of finance and industry. His macroeconomic vision elucidates that the allocation of liquidity, the income distribution and social welfare are not only the result of market forces and industrial processes, but principally of cultural forces. This emphasis on the role of culture as a factor that shapes macroeconomic behaviour brings about significant conceptual implications. Economic policy-making is fashioned within actual cultural circumstances in the fields of finance, technology, industry and politics. Changes in economic policy ensue from the cultural coherence or incoherence that prevails among the various sub-systems in the complex and evolving economic and social structure. In this setting, the acceptance of Veblen's holistic macroeconomic perspective justifies a program of reform and a policy strategy along the following fundamental principles: business processes and pecuniary institutions undermine equity, efficiency and stability. Evolving pecuniary institutions increase financial complexity and fragility and endogenously generate destabilising processes so that depressions and cyclical fluctuations appear as natural consequences of the business enterprise system. Financial institutions and tangible investment financing cannot be left to unregulated financial markets. The elimination of waste requires an efficient allocation of financial resources and protection against predatory instincts, habits and routines in business and banking. Institutionally legitimised workmanship is necessary if industrial efficiency and community's welfare are to be at the epicentre of economic policy. Government spending increases financial stability and welfare because it fills the spending gaps in the private-enterprise economy. A higher aggregate demand supports employment, income flows and solvency.

Conclusions

Veblen's thinking about economic policy offers no final words, but it has considerable and enduring intellectual value. Veblen maintained, contrary to the habitual postulated principles of the orthodox economic theory, that the capitalist system is not self-adjusting. The pecuniary nature of financial institutions is primarily responsible for the lack of automatic adjustment to a full employment social welfare. He was among the first economists who repudiated laissez-faire and illuminated the flaws and limitations of the business enterprise system. He uncovered the liquidity allocation and income distribution inefficiencies and insufficient demand as the major shortfalls of the business enterprise system. Financial fragility and instability and debt-deflation were among the reasons why he rejected the self-adjusting nature of a capitalist economy. These insights form the pragmatic basis of his proposal for government and central bank interventions.

Veblen illustrated that the growth of finance is an ongoing cultural complex process of habits, ideas, attitudes and beliefs that institutionalise financial routines that structure the wealthy class-biased frame of mind of those engaged in economic policy-making. From this viewpoint, the macroeconomic system and the economic policy-making ultimately depend on cultural processes that exercise powerful and enduring influence over the realms of finance, technology and industry and on their close entwines. The governing habits of mind do not encourage investment in productive capital assets. Investment decisions and attitudes change as the institutional process of forming habits, norms and customs progress. Financing, position-making and the building of leverage structures bring with them habits of thought that are compatible with manipulation, speculation, inefficiency, inequality and insufficient demand. Parasitic investment and finance deters full employment, equity and economic growth.

Significant institutional and policy implications arise from Veblen's cultural, holistic macroeconomics. A new institutional structure is needed in order to promote the instinct of workmanship. Macroeconomic management should activate productive expenditures and create possibilities that could advance employment and prosperity. The elimination of wasteful consumption and emulation necessitates distributional changes and supposes the necessity of habits, norms and patterns of consumption and investment that augment tangible assets and increase expenditures for serviceable output. But, community will attain a higher welfare only under a certain cultural setting conducive to technology and the state of the industrial arts. For Veblen, not all institutions and policy interventions are growth and welfare enhancing. He proclaimed the need to build up processes, routines and habits of thought that promote the instinct of workmanship. This is the necessary precondition for a higher level of community's welfare. But, this can happen only if the industrial system is controlled and managed by the social groups of technicians, engineers, scientists and workers.

Veblen regarded the institution of absentee ownership as fundamental for macroeconomic evolution. He proclaimed that the interest of managers lies in the stability of the market value of good-will and the making of large pecuniary profits. Veblen condemned pecuniary efficiency as an institutional flaw of capitalism. His pessimistic perspective on economic and social issues revealed that in his social philosophy, capitalism even rightly organised, it would be, most likely, more efficient, but still highly intolerable on ethical grounds. This probably explains the political basis of Veblen's consistent attacks upon the evolving financial habits and routines and institutional foundations of this system, which render indistinguishable its predatory and productive configurations.

Closing, the general perspective from which Veblen projected policy insights was that of his post-Darwinian macroeconomic theory. The essence of this theory is a criticism of parasitic, finance capitalism, combined with a desire to establish an institutional environment in which a workmanship-led industrial system, however preferably without private property, can function. In this regard, Veblen overwhelmingly rejected the *status quo*.

Notes

1 Veblen (1919) defined the net product as the amount by which the actual production exceeds its own cost, which is counted in terms of subsistence and the cost of the mechanical equipment. For a more detailed analysis of Veblen's analysis of productive capacity, actual production and net product, see Gruchy (1958) and Dente (1977).

2 At this point, it is worth noting Veblen's (1904) comment on Hobson's thesis on under-consumption and remedies to cope with it. Hobson proposed the reform of the distribution of consuming power by imposing higher taxes on unearned incomes, higher wages and shorter working day. Veblen seemed to endorse these propositions, but he was concerned about their feasibility, since, as he argued, economic policy is guided by business interests.

3 The discussion which follows involves primarily Veblen's demand-side remedies. But, it is important to stress that his analysis also incorporates supply-side interventions and practices that the business sector uses to avoid profit realisation problems and depression, such as protective tariffs to lessen foreign competition, and collusive strategies to curtail the output produced and to manipulate goods price (see e.g. Reines and Leathers, 2008).

4 See e.g. Dillard (1980; 1987) and Wray (2007a).

5 Dente (1977) argued that Veblen's aggregative analysis and national economic accounts made him a pioneer in national income economics.

6 Veblen did not incorporate parasitic household debt in his 'financial instability hypothesis'. If such concerns are taken into consideration, then the even higher share

of conspicuous consumption will further amplify the discrepancy between actual and perspective profits and increase the solvency risk for corporations. This ramification in parallel with the higher unemployment rate that reduces wages and the income flows for households increases the likelihood of financial fragility.

7   Raines and Leathers (2008, p. 56) noted that "the most important new development in corporate finance was the emergence of the large investment bankers, as exemplified and personified by J.P. Morgan".

3 Unsustainable asset and liability structures, market processes and Minsky's macroeconomics

Introduction

Minsky envisaged an evolutionary, finance-driven theory to explain macro-economic change in market economies. This theory elucidates that the evolution of the macro-system is a continuous process of adaptation to changes in the financial structure of effective demand. The latter is predisposed to speculative and Ponzi leverage structures and failed margins of safety, which normally emanate from unregulated borrowing and lending practices in the corporate, banking, household and government sectors. In addition, Minsky's macro-theory brings to surface the market processes through which financial entrepreneurship and financial innovation and competition originate risky techniques in the financing of capital asset ownership, household spending and asset holding inducing financial fragility and instability and debt deflation.

In this chapter, I present the most useful of Minsky's insights that, in my viewpoint, constitute his contribution to the building of evolutionary foundations for macroeconomics.[1] It will be argued that the essence of Minsky's macroeconomic theory is the illumination of the micro-meso[2] financial processes that, in a debt-driven 'Wall Street' model of capitalism, make an economy's financial structure sometimes stable and robust and sometimes fragile and unstable. Attention is paid to how these financial processes govern production, prices, income distribution and effective demand. A significant element of Minsky's core theoretical structure is the coordination failure between cash inflows and cash outflows, which stem from productive operations, position-making[3] activities and adjustments in portfolio compositions. Of interest, too, is that Minsky's evolutionary financial macro-vision adds significant analytical value to a more pragmatic understanding of the cause and effect of financialisation in contemporary capitalist economies.

The foundations of Minsky's evolutionary finance: Schumpeter and Keynes

Minsky's financial macroeconomic theory constitutes a significant contribution to the neo-Schumpeterian evolutionary theorisation. The neo-Schumpeterian tradition has certainly founded a sophisticated supply-side-driven and, pre-dominantly, an industrial innovation-driven approach to economic evolution.[4] Development and change are anticipated as cumulative processes that are ruled by the response of knowledge-based organisations to continuous changes in industrial entrepreneurship, technology, innovation and organisational structures. Minsky acknowledged the contribution of the abovementioned 'real' forces to economic development. Nevertheless, he maintained that in finance capitalism, economic evolution should be principally scrutinised in the light of the evolving financial institutions and the structural changes in financial markets. For this reason, Minsky (1986a; 1990) proclaimed that there is a gap of realism in the neo-Schumpeterian perspective due to its incompetence to contemplate the financial factors that govern change in financially sophisticated market economies. In his opinion, the functioning, coherence and change of modern economies are dominated by the dynamics of capital development under systemic uncertainty and by the complex network of financial interrelations and cash flows, which influence the funding and financing of private investment. Given the fact that such dynamics comprise short-term fluctuations as well as long-term transformations, Minsky (1986a, p. 113) proposed the construction of a more realistic conceptual framework, which would integrate "Schumpeter's insights with regard to the dynamics of a capitalist process and the role of innovative entrepreneurs into an analytical framework that in its essential properties is Keynesian". This conception, as Whalen (2001) observed, is associated with his endeavour to explore a historical and institutional perspective of the 'Wall Street' model of American capitalism.[5]

For Minsky, Schumpeter's theory of economic development is a valuable source of insights to comprehend the behaviour of a fully integrated and profit-seeking entrepreneurial economy and the resilience of market economies. But, on the other hand, Minsky (1975a) argued that Keynes's *General Theory* provides financial foundations to comprehend an integrated monetary-production economy. Nevertheless, he endorsed that Keynes's vision is more precise and analytical than Schumpeter's vision, because it contextualises a monetary structure to consider the fragility and instability of a 'Wall Street' market economy. In Minsky's (1982, p. 60) words, "in the *General Theory*, Keynes developed a theory of the capitalist process which was able to explain financial and output instability as the result of market behaviour in the face of uncertainty". Moreover, he upheld that in Keynes's 'Wall Street' paradigm, economic units make use of money so as to join in market processes, to deal with uncertainty and to remain solvent and liquid. Keynes's monetary conceptions qualified Minsky to think about the financial market processes that bring to the fore money and finance in the valuation of capital assets and in the determination of the price of current output. On these grounds, Minsky endeavoured to deploy how financial market processes induce endogenous forces that destabilise the financial system and the macroeconomic order. Note that for Minsky (1986b), the incorporation of institutions, such as money and finance, in economic analysis deemphasises macroeconomics as a study of Walrasian/Hicksian general equilibrium and leads to a consideration of the evolving institutional reality of the inherently unstable capitalist economies.

In this vein, Minsky capitalised on the incorporation of Schumpeter's insights of entrepreneurship, innovation and competition in Keynes's monetary system. His determination enabled him to conceptually integrate Keynes's analysis of business cycles and of financial interrelations with endogenous Schumpeterian-type creative destruction processes in finance. The enduring value of this integration is that it contextualises the role of money and finance in economic evolution. Minsky (1986a, p. 121) clarified his scientific purpose by arguing that a useful economic theory, which enables us to comprehend structural evolution and transformation, must integrate "Schumpeter's vision of a resilient intertemporal capitalist process with Keynes's hard insights into the fragility introduced into the capitalist accumulation process by some inescapable properties of capitalist financial structure". I should note that for Minsky, the usefulness of such an economic theory is that it mixes the industrial sector with the financial sector, thereby creating a complex, time dependent and evolving macro-system. Minsky (1990, p. 58) was very certain about how to accomplish this mixing. He stated that

> if we add Keynes's theory of asset prices as a capitalisation of expected profits, where the capitalisation rate reflects portfolio opportunities, to the Schumpeter view that the function of banking is to determine the investment ideas that become investment projects, we are on our way to integrating Schumpeter and Keynes.

Besides, he commented that monetary and financial factors cannot be incorporated into an initially given 'real' model, as the Walrasian tradition does. Only a theory that integrates financial relations, which involve the financing of positions in financial and real assets, into its basic construction can explain why capitalism exhibits both fragility and resiliency over its historical progress (Ferri and Minsky, 1991).

Minsky (1990, p. 61) fully recognised that Schumpeter, himself, designated banks and finance as important determinants of firms' capacity to get resources necessary to initiate new technological innovations and competition in industry. He remarked that "the essential point of Schumpeter's view of money and banks is that new combinations in production and new products could not appear without being financed: finance and development are in a symbiotic relation". Nonetheless, he notified that although finance is at the centre of Schumpeter's theory of development, it is the industrial sector that eventually appears as being capable of technological advance and of knowledge absorption. Most importantly, Schumpeter considered the role of money and finance only in the realisation of monetary profit-seeking activities in industry. Minsky emphasised that Schumpeter's evolutionary vision is limited to industrial technology and organisation capabilities, as the neo-Schumpeterian tradition habitually does. However, in such a case, the role of money and finance in economic change demotes. But, for Minsky (1986a, p. 117), Schumpeter claimed that money itself in not an outside asset but it is introduced into the economy in a financing transaction which, in the abstract case of no government and household debts, is a transaction that finances investment output and ownership of capital assets.

The above passage suggests that Minsky, indeed, believed that money and finance are essential in the Schumpeterian process of development. Therefore, economic theory inescapably needs to integrate these institutions into its basic formulation from the beginning, as Keynes did when he introduced money into the determination of the price level of capital assets.[6] This, for Minsky, is entirely necessary if we want to distinguish between an evolutionary theory from a non-evolutionary and static mainstream theory, which is extraordinarily non-monetary. However, in Schumpeter's vision, creative destruction processes and macroeconomic instability are normal results of combination failures of industrial entrepreneurial activity and capital accumulation. Therefore, despite the fact that Schumpeter considered banking to be a full partner in economic evolution and development, he undervalued the key role of entrepreneurship, innovation and competition in finance and banking. Minsky (1986a, p. 121) believed that "Schumpeter got enmeshed in a Walrasian trap that assumed only real things matter, whereas in his official vision money mattered". For this reason, Minsky appraised Schumpeter's vision as incomplete to establish the foundations of a macro-finance approach to economic evolution in accordance with, his own financial interpretation of, Keynes's *General Theory*.

The shortcomings of Schumpeter's monetary analysis inspired Minsky to scrutinise the role of finance and banking within his stage theory of capitalist development.[7] Minsky upheld that the development of capitalism evidences that finance increasingly 'rules the roost' and industry takes a back seat in the continuing search for monetary profit. The incorporation of financial entrepreneurship, innovation and competition into Keynes's 'Wall Street Paradigm' enabled him to scrutinise the cause and effect of evolutionary finance. Following Schumpeter, Minsky (1986a; 1990) proclaimed that economic development requires the redeployment of inherited capital. Banks are indispensable in the process of economic evolution, because they mediate in the redeployment process by redirecting their liquidity reserves as debts are repaid. Monetary profit-seeking entrepreneurs in the banking sector create innovations that principally take either the form of new assets available for households or of new ways of financing business investment. Minsky (1990, p. 5) grasped this insight as an essential point of compatibility of the visions of Schumpeter and Keynes, as banks emerge to involve into the endogenous creation of money supply. In his logic, financial innovation and competition constitute a selection mechanism that rules the evolution of financial contracts, relations and structures and of endogenous processes of money supply that create potentialities for continuous and cumulative layering and higher burdens of payments.

Moreover, the financing of innovations in industry increases the cash flows interdependence of economic units. There are two crucial aspects behind the impact of financial innovations on financial complexity and diversity: the funds the financial institutions make available to manufacturing firms in order to engage in the competitive industrial process of creative destruction and the competitive forces of creative destruction in finance that create leverage and liability structures. One of Minsky's most useful observations is that banks' endogenous processes of money supply encourage layering and higher burdens of payments that raise solvency, liquidity and default risks for monetary and non-monetary organisations. As indicated in detail below, these effects depend on the coordination of cash flows, which determine the quality of the leverage structure created by the layering of liabilities. On this ground, Burlamaqui and Kregel (2005) notified that in order to comprehend the destabilising role of finance, it is important to consider the evolution from Schumpeter's into Minsky's view of banking, that is from a passive institution that finances manufacturing innovation and growth to one that aggressively innovate to increase liquidity and profitability. Schumpeter's banks require knowledge on the clients, the production cost and market conditions to supply loans to their customers, while Minsky's banks require complex information about the price formation and variation in securities markets.

Financial innovation improves the performance of financial institutions not only in ongoing struggles to survive, but also in creating new products and hence prospects for higher profits and market shares. In this line of institutional analysis, Minsky envisioned that there is significant complexity and variation within the banking system. The reason is, as Burlamaqui and Kregel (2005, p. 14) argued, that

> banks compete differently depending on the state of their own balance sheets and the state of the economy as a whole. When financial institutions are competing aggressively, they seek to maximise their market share; but when faced with difficulties they restrict their market expansion and compete for liquidity and/or solvency.

For Minsky, the behaviour of innovating financial entrepreneurs and banking competition explains Keynes's apprehension of the restructuring in balance sheets in calendar time. Detection of balance-sheet problems by investors could have severe repercussions for a bank's – and a firm's – solvency and credit rating. The possibility of a shortfall of cash flows or of a change in financing terms prompts revisions to solvency risk, the market value of capital assets and to investment plans. Banks that face balance-sheet problems do not lend money to firms and other financial institutions, particularly when the latter are deemed as being insolvent. Minsky drew certain attention to the fact that innovation and competition in banking are factors that cause an underestimation of risks when, as noted below, the economy expands and there is an overestimation of risks when the economy contracts. Minsky (1992a) notified that money-fund managers would amplify these tendencies because they diversify their portfolios rapidly and globally, deterring productive and income creation processes. In any case, if there is a shortfall of cash flows, the survival of firms and banks will depend on their effective use of leverage.

Micro-financial failures: insufficient liquidity and coordination failures of cash flows

The essence of Minsky's evolutionary macro-vision revolves around the presumption that any organisation employing high leverage would be sensitive to changes in solvency and liquidity risks, and to signs of a drop in cash inflows and in asset prices. The act of deleveraging is the most effective form of self-defence and surviving. But deleveraging would have many meso-macro repercussions because it affects all units involved in an economy's complex financial structure. Minsky pointed out that financial institutions, alike non-financial corporate firms, households and governments, face a 'survival constraint'. It is worthy of note that the 'survival constraint' is one of the most useful conceptions of Minsky's macro-vision, because it elucidates that aggregate demand is predisposed to solvency risk and to a potentially fragile and unsustainable financial structure. The 'survival constraint' influences units' financing and spending decision-making, if their cash flows and existing position in assets cannot be maintained.

For Minsky (1982), the 'survival constraint' requires that cash outflow, which is necessary to maintain the liabilities created to acquire assets must not exceed cash inflow created by the same stock of assets, if organisations' solvency is to be sustained. A maturity mismatch between assets and liabilities on the balance sheets of firms and banks is likely to generate coordination failures of cash inflows and cash outflows, and liquidity and solvency risks for some units whose quality of leverage and liability structures would decrease. In this regard, Burlamaqui (2000) and Burlamaqui and Kregel (2005) marked out that financial markets, relations and linkages are imperative for a market economy, because they construct a liquidity structure that oxygenates units. The available liquidity enables units to spend without having savings and, most importantly, to refinance their positions and to serve inherited debt commitments. Nonetheless, cumulative debt-driven spending and refinancing is likely to cause over-leverage and to increase the likelihood economic units, in due course, to become insolvent. Minsky claimed that this is even more possible to occur during economic euphoria, when units customarily had formed overoptimistic cash inflow expectations that failed to be confirmed. But, insolvency may induce liquidity crunches, which, in turn, increase the possibility of units facing conditions of default and bankruptcy.

Moreover, the 'survival constraint' designates the capability of firms to effectively cope with uncertainty. On the ground of Keynes's conception of fundamental uncertainty (Davidson, 1978) and of the inherent volatility of asset prices, Burlamaqui (2000, p. 15) argued that "liquidity provides a crucial protective device or defensive to manage uncertainty". Burlamaqui and Kregel (2005, p. 12) notified that firms and banks make use of liquidity to deal with uncertainty, because the value of money is less volatile than of the value of other financial assets and consequently "it provides assurance that future cash commitments can be met with certainty". Accordingly, the desire of economic units to hold cash cushions constitutes a rational choice, at a micro level, to avoid liquidity crunches and solvency risk. This choice becomes even more important for banks and other financial institutions. The reason is that for Minsky, banks are cash flow machines. If their cushion of safety declines, the likelihood to become incapable of meeting cash flow commitments increases. In addition, if a bank is solvent, it provides assurance to markets that it is able to deal with liquidity risk, and *vice versa*.

In Minsky's system, financial institutions survive if they are regularly innovated by applying new product and new combinations and processes that create liquidity to exploit market opportunities. However, as Minsky (1975a) notified, their capacity to increase their assets depends on the solvency of financial and non-financial private units to supply acceptable and sustainable liabilities, when they build up leverage structures. It is important to underline that intensive innovation and competition increase financial complexity and the likelihood of maturity mismatches between assets and liabilities. This then increases uncertainty in financial markets regarding the coordination of cash flows. The increasing reliance of organisations on refinancing sources and asset liquidation procedures so as to fulfil debt commitments decreases the quality of their leverage. Therefore, banks and other financial institutions accrue information to form expectations about the existing market prices and the solvency rating of the participants in financial markets. Given that there is no reliable information about an uncertain future, an effective coordination between cash inflow and cash outflow becomes systemically unlikely for banks and units engaged in profit-making and innovation creating processes. By noting this principle, Minsky proclaimed the plausibility of insolvency and of liquidity crunches, unless, as noted below, the central bank would intervene to create inflationary liabilities in an attempt to control the endogenous forces that induce coordination failures of cash flows.

Consequently, in Minsky's macro-vision, financial innovation and competition rule the interaction and competition among financial institutions and between financial and non-financial organisations when they build structures of assets and liabilities. The ability of banks to make sustainable profits and stay solvent and liquid relies upon their organisational capacity to successfully carry on new innovations, and on their risk and return. The competitive game among financial institutions influences the allocation of liquidity, which ultimately drives the allocation of monetary profits among organisations. However, monetary profits are income and liquidity inflows for organisations. A downward pressure on profits and, hence, on cash inflows brings about variety and diversity in the anticipation of solvency risk, which makes complex the process of detection of an organisation's appropriate margins of safety. Besides, Minsky pinpointed that the sustainability of cash inflows is uncertain, because financial competition stimulates imitation strategies that encourage risky financial practices and innovations. However, as argued below, the impact of the aforementioned micro-financial dynamics becomes dependent upon the meso–macro environment, which will amplify or dampen the impact that risky micro-financial routines and practices exert on the quality of an economy's financial structure.

This insight, which directly marks the co-evolution between the financial and macroeconomic systems, led Minsky to pay particular attention to the routine of securitisation as an innovative financing technique. Minsky (1987a) argued that in managed money capitalism, securitisation and 'off-balance sheet' operations bring about the decline of regulated banks and financial institutions in the allocation of liquidity, while they broaden the role of unregulated money-managing institutions and financial markets. This institutional transformation of the banking system has further encouraged risk-taking behaviour, speculative practices and the creation of risky financial products that increase systemic risk. These effects transformed banking towards the so called 'originate and distribute' model, which downgrades risk and, as Kregel (2008) noted, the cushions of safety. Minsky associated securitisation with his 'money manager' stage of capitalism, in which almost unregulated pension funds, hedge funds and sovereign wealth funds speculatively use a large pool of liquidity to make high, short-term profits. Minsky (1987a) endorsed that securitisation makes the dealings and connections between units and financial markets more complex, uncertain and fragile. The reason is that money-managing institutions use securitisation to create credit that does not absorb high-power money and hence there is no recourse to bank capital. As a result, securitisation accelerates the rate of growth of private debt relative to income from productive activity. In addition, it induces units to make position by selling position. This development has been further boosted by the influence of money managers on business leaders to devote attention principally to shareholder value (Whalen, 2017). But, over-leverage, together with banks' incapability to identify appropriate margins of safety, boosts uncertainty about the refinancing capacity of speculative and especially Ponzi units to meet payment commitments and about the sustainability of the solvency of their liability structures. Minsky (1970) observed that these destabilising processes, induced by financial innovations, are more likely to occur during economic euphoria, because bankers and money managers change conventions and their view about the business-cycle effect on the present value of profits, cash flows and asset prices. Throughout his writings, Minsky repeatedly commented that the layering of debt on debt increases the fragility of the financial system and the possibility of financial instability and crisis.

Accordingly, for Minsky, there is a continuous and cumulative dynamic interplay principally between the business and financial sectors. The original aspect of Minsky's integration of Schumpeter and Keynes is that financial fragility and macroeconomic instability 'naturally' emanate from financial entrepreneurship and processes that create innovations in finance. Financial competition drives entrepreneurship to pro-cyclically increase leverage and approve riskier practices in order to maintain market shares and make higher monetary gains. But such behaviour provokes an over-creation of liabilities that increase the possibility of coordination failures of cash flows. This outcome raises the thrust towards financial instability and amplifies an economy's business-cycle tendency. Minsky disclosed the endogenous financial processes of macroeconomic instability that are grounded in the impact of risky portfolio adjustments on the quality of the financial structure of effective demand. In this vein, Minsky (1986b, p. 266–267) argued that banking literature posits the concept of the prudent banker: a banker who accepts just the right amount of risk. To a banker risk results from the selection of assets, liabilities, and leverage, that is, from the composition of the balance sheet. But the risks bankers carry are not objective probability phenomena; instead they are uncertainty relations that are subjectively valued.

Banker's risky business and solvency illusions together with uncertainty and financial complexity affect the volume and the micro-allocation of liquidity. But, risky lending practices increase the possibility of mismatching cash inflow and cash outflow and of solvency risk. Banks' solvency illusions result from changes in the state of confidence regarding the expected cash flows, price of assets and value of collaterals. However, solvency illusions may ultimately oblige financial institutions to deleverage. This then would affect the decisions of units to make new positions in real capital and financial assets influencing the cyclical behaviour of prices, income, employment and economic growth. In this regard, Minsky upheld that explosive business cycles rather than steady growth are the normal result of the complex process of financial innovation and competition. For him, the evolution of finance dominates the relations of production and distribution and affects the stability and coherence of market economies.

Mental models and meso-financial processes

Minsky's key macro-contention is that the relation between the various sources and uses of cash held by various classes of economic units (business firms, households, financial institutions, government) determines the endogenous dynamics of capitalist economies. Macroeconomic evolution takes place because financial innovation and competition alter the financing and funding practices of units, especially during economic euphoria. Minsky presumed that the restructuring of portfolios contains speculative and risky decisions about which assets the units to get hold of and how to finance their obtainment. For instance, financial institutions engender financing commitments because they hold assets that are negotiable in financial markets and have credit lines at other banks. In a complex financial structure, and given Keynes's fundamental uncertainty, financing and funding are processes that configure organisations' capacity to manage the coordination of cash flows. From this conception, it becomes profound that the evolving financial structure of organisations hinges upon the micro-dynamics of cash receipts and payments over a period of time. Minsky (1993) presumed that at the micro level, units' rationally endeavour to deal with the coordination between their cash receipts and payments. But, he asserted that this micro-rationality cannot resolve the coordination failure of cash flows at the meso-macro levels.

Minsky (1996, p. 360) acknowledged that the origin of this coordination failure is that agents construct mental models that guide their actions on the ground of "their place in the economy, their history, and their ability to generalise and abstract". As a result, there are different mental models that guide agents' actual decisions, which induce significant diversity in the processes of forming expectations about the risk and return of various assets and liability structures. The same holds when agents form expectations in relation to major macro-variables.[8] In addition, Minsky, (1996, p. 358) remarked that

> agents need to learn the model of the economy they use in decision-making and that the complexity of economic processes and the time consuming nature of learning means that the agents are never sure of the validity of the models they use.

All Minsky is saying is that given the evolving financial and macroeconomic conditions, the mental models that rule units' action are very likely to disregard the factors that currently drive the formation of expectations and actions. Besides, Minsky (1995a) observed that agents' risk is endogenously determined. In his analysis, a profit-seeking behaviour by economic agents is affected by their experience.

Tymoigne (2006) notified that, in Minsky's system, experiences from economic success attenuate risk aversion, while experiences from economic failure increase risk aversion. This diversity is attenuated by the prevailing conventions, which order the tolerable practices used by financial institutions in the building of asset and liability structures. What is more interesting in Minsky's argument is that conventions, apart from the formation of expectations, rule units' confidence in setting the margins of safety when they engage in lending and borrowing practices. But conventions and confidence change as an economy evolves, especially during periods of prolonged economic growth and rapid financial innovations. Over-confidence leads to over-optimism in the sustainability of the expected cash inflows and in the quality of liability structures. In contrast, when uncertainty increases, changes in conventions may reduce confidence, which, in turn, triggers the need, especially for banks, to reset the tolerable margins of safety. Therefore, conventions, variations in major macro-variables, and continuous and cumulative layering of liabilities compose Minsky's complex and evolving financial macroeconomic structure, which affects and is affected by coordination failures of cash flows.

It is worth noting that throughout his writings, Minsky introduced the idea that an effective evaluation of organisations' solvency risk and margins of safety requires a cash-flow-based bank examination method that involves a banking approach for all units. He upheld that this examination method illuminates the meso-macro ramifications of the micro-dynamics of a mismatch between cash inflows and cash outflows. Minsky and Campbell (1988, p. 255) emphasised that this examination method analyses

> the structure of balance sheets, payment commitments and position-making activities. Position-making for a bank consists of the transactions undertaken to bring the cash position to the level required by regulation or bank management. In the position-making view, bank failures do not arise simply because of incompetent or corrupt management. They occur

mainly because of the interdependence of payment commitments and position making transactions across institutions and units.

His concern was to use this examination method to generate information on the liquidity and solvency risks of particular organisations. But, in his analysis of the speculative practices, especially in financing and funding of positions in capital assets, Minsky recognised that their destabilising impact becomes dependent upon the liquidity conditions and the order of financial markets. This notion enabled him to conceptualise the preconditions of financial order and stability at the meso-macro level, and, especially, to recognise the necessity of a central bank, which is better informed, to monitor the micro-dynamics of cash flows. But, as he regularly pinpointed, such a central bank must first acknowledge the possibility of coordination failures of cash flows. Note that in this approach, the emphasis is on the capability of banks and of the central bank to monitor the complex, uncertain and evolving position-making activities of units and to detect risky contractual interrelations among banks and between banks and non-bank financial institutions. This observation is an original constituent of Minsky's core evolutionary macro-vision, which brings to light the limits of stabilising the evolving and financially unstable market economies.

Furthermore, for Minsky, the order and stability of financial markets are decisive because they rule units' refinancing capacity at the meso level. An uninterrupted refinancing is fundamental for all units to manage the coordination of cash flows at the micro level. Minsky's meso-analysis brings to the fore the macro-importance of solvency. According to Minsky, a unit is solvent when its net worth is positive. But net worth is derived by the market valuation of a unit's assets and liabilities. A unit is liquid when it can meet its payment commitments. Minsky claimed that in order to protect solvency, units have a tendency to demand assets that reduce liquidity risk and offer protection against a liquidity crisis or temporarily disorganised asset markets. Minsky (1970, p. 27) maintained that "liquidity preference is defined as a rational person's demand for money as an asset; this leads to a determinate demand function for money for any value of higher order uncertainty". In addition, Minsky (1970, p. 27) accentuated that

> the risk averter reaction to a decline in confidence is to attempt to increase the weight of assets that yield flexibility in portfolio choices, in other words, to increase the value not only of money but also of assets that have broad, deep and resilient markets.

Solvency and liquidity are two conditions that all units must constantly satisfy in order to preserve the status of their creditworthiness in financial markets.

In another passage, Minsky (1975b, p. 153) blended his micro and meso perceptions of liquidity. He marked out that liquidity is not an innate attribute of an asset, but rather that liquidity is a time-related characteristic of an ongoing, continuing economic institution imbedded in an evolving financial system. Whether a particular institution is, or is not, liquid over some time horizon depends not only upon its initial balance sheet, but also upon what happens in its business operations as well as in the various financial markets in which the instruments it owns or sells are traded.

The business operations generate income creation and distribution processes that deliver income and cash inflows. However, as stated earlier, once the cash inflows cannot get together with the cash outflows required by the unit's liability structure, a need for additional cash appears. A unit can adjust its need for cash by position-making activities that vitally depend on the expected liquidity conditions in various financial markets. Kregel (2014, p. 6) stressed that Minsky distinguished between 'position liquidity' and 'market liquidity' to locate the "dual vulnerability emerging whenever cash flows from normal operations are insufficient to meet financial commitments". The same holds whenever a unit is unable to sell assets or to issue debt to raise cash.

As noted above, a unit's cash inflows, which are the basis for the valuation of its net worth, depend upon an economy's meso-macro conditions. In Minsky's (1967, p. 2) words

> any statement about a unit's liquidity, therefore depends upon estimating how its normal activities under which its assets (including its ability to borrow as an 'honorary' asset) can be transformed into cash... Any statement about the liquidity of an institution depends upon assumptions about the behaviour of the economy and financial markets. As the assumptions are changed, the estimate of the liquidity of the institutions will vary.

Thus, any evaluation about the solvency and liquidity risks of an organisation is susceptible to the evolving meso-macro environments, and in particular, to the order and stability of financial markets and to the level of aggregate demand. If meso-macro conditions change, conventions and confidence over the available liquidity change and, hereafter, the evaluation of the quality of a unit's balance sheet will vary. At the micro level, the 'survival constraint' dictates an organisation, which does not have an idle cash balance, to have net cash inflows to avoid insolvency and default. Nevertheless, an organisation's failure to satisfy the interconnected solvency and liquidity risks might open a solvency hole in other units' balance sheets. The process of detecting balance-sheet problems by investors can have severe repercussions for units' creditworthiness and credit rating. If banks cut off units' access to liquidity lines, they will make them unable to fulfil debt obligations. This effect would increase systemic risk and fragility. Besides, if they, eventually, default, or begin deleveraging, the macroeconomy would lose significant sources of spending and income creation processes.

Minsky's 'financial instability hypothesis'

Minsky's 'financial instability hypothesis' (hereafter MFIH) is the heart of his macro-vision. I have argued (Argitis, 2017) that MFIH is a significant contribution to the development of a broader Schumpeterian theorising of macroeconomic evolution. It describes how Schumpeterian processes of creation and destruction in finance affect resource creation processes and the co-evolution between the financial system and the macro-system; and depicts the key role of the micro-meso-macro inter-connectedness among units' cash flow contractual commitments and solvency, the order of financial markets and policy institutions. MFIH elucidates how evolutionary finance erodes the macroeconomic coherence of market economies.

More specifically, Minsky (1970; 1986b) maintained that the coherence of an evolving macro-system depends on the growth of the layering of unsustainable liability structures and on the growth of the realised effective demand. He defined financial fragility and macroeconomic incoherence on the ground of the proportion of income transactions to the balance-sheet transactions and portfolio transactions. He distinguished between these three types of transactions in order to detect the evolving solvency regime of a unit and the possibility of a systemic financial disorder. Minsky perceived the normal source of cash inflows for all organisations the income arises from production and distribution processes.[9] Cash inflows to make payments on liabilities might also arise – especially for banks and financial institutions – from refinancing of positions that is from selling assets and emitting new liabilities. Liquidating inherited assets is the third possible way for organisations to obtain cash. It is worth noting that Minsky drew special attention to payments that involve the guarantee of collateral. In his argument, these payments are pivotal because they correlate the market value of collateral with units' capability to make cash payments and their need for additional liquidity, whenever the market value of collateral falls below a threshold.

Minsky proclaimed that over a prolonged, and especially a euphoric, expansion, the balance-sheet commitments – i.e. interest and repayment of principal – are likely to increase faster than income receipts from income production and distribution processes. As a result, leverage would increase faster than income and subsequently the sum of financial commitments would upsurge relative to income, especially if debt is not used to expand a firm's productive capacity. Note that Minsky exemplified this conception by arguing that slow or negative growth rates reduce cash inflows and strengthen units' coordination failure of cash flows. In this case, portfolio payments might increase relative to both income and financial transactions, because organisations, which habitually use income cash flows to meet their financial commitments, find themselves in the urgent need of refinancing their position. In this vein, liquidity pressures are placed upon financial institutions and financial markets. Minsky was well aware of the possibility that a considerable drop in the price of assets will activate negative changes in net worth and the market value of collateral. This holds not only for the selling organisations, but for all organisations holding those assets in portfolios. In disorder and illiquid markets, the abovementioned consequence renders units incompetent to raise the required cash. This meso-destabilising process can be interrupted only if, as argued in detail in the next chapter, the traded assets are protected and their prices are stabilised by central bank's refinancing positions at the macro level. In this manner, the solvency of organisations at micro-meso levels and the sustainability of an economy's financial structure depend on changes in units' net worth and the ratio of the value of unprotected to protected assets. The relative prices of assets change along with portfolio transformations. Portfolio adjustments occur whenever the established conventions in lending and borrowing practices change, uncertainty increases and solvency illusions collapse.

Most importantly, portfolio adjustments that result from a lack of confidence over the future state of macroeconomy induce shifts towards assets that offer protection against large declines in nominal values. Units, especially banks, prefer to hold assets that reduce liquidity risk and the possibility of a liquidity crisis. The risk increases when the quantity of investment rises, because banks and firms become conscious of higher risk associated with over-leverage. The reason is that banks consider borrowers' and their own balance sheets and leveraging capital as net worth and prospective income flows. In this regard, as Kregel (1997; 2007) and Papadimitriou and Wray (1998) argued, they use informal rules of thumb to value the margins of safety. Note that the quality of an economy's financial structure, ultimately, depends on the scale the assets created are protected and default free assets or unprotected and default possible assets. By remarking on this principle, Minsky argued that in a euphoric, and especially unregulated, economy, the level of such protection decreases, and hence, financial macroeconomic instability is very likely to evidence.

In this financial setting, Minsky underlined the importance of income cash flows, because they define the sustainability of the solvency status of a unit. As already stated, the available liquidity becomes dependent upon the margins of safety that are embodied in the cash flows dynamics of units. In the context of Minsky's 'cash box condition', Tymoigne (2006, p. 17) argued that the margins of safety corresponds to

> the expected existence of a positive net cash inflow on income and balance sheet operations, the expected capacity to increase cash at low cost from portfolio operations (speculation and position making) and the existence of a comfortable idle amount of cash and superfluous liquid assets that limits the expected need to liquidate a strategic position.

Nevertheless, position-making operations build leverage structures that in turn create liability structures, which will be validated or repudiated by the subsequent operation of the economy and the flow of liquidity to organisations. Minsky (1986b) asserted that an economy's financial structure can be distinguished by its degree of robustness and fragility. The classification of a financial structure as robust or fragile depends on the relation between organisations' cash flows, i.e. profits, wages, taxes and cash flows from owned assets,[10] and the payment commitments determined by their liability structures. He stated that this classification hinges on the mix of his three, well-known, solvency regimes, namely, hedge, speculative and Ponzi. Each of these regimes is determined by the dynamics that emanate from cash inflows from income production and distribution processes and the cash outflows due to balance sheet and portfolio transactions.

For hedge units, the cash flows from income production and sale of output operations are expected to be adequately large to meet the contractual payments on account of both interest and principal on its liabilities during every period over an extended horizon. Besides, the larger the equity share, which does not commit payments, in a unit's financial structure, the higher the possibility that the unit is a hedge financing unit. Equity and long-term debt financing are features of hedge units, which are solvent and do not depend on raising funds in financial markets to fulfil their obligations. Therefore, there is no need to make positions. For speculative units the present value of expected cash flows earned from income and balance-sheet operations are adequate to pay the interest on debts, but are inadequate to fulfil the payments due on the principal of its maturing liabilities. But, because liabilities are more current than assets, refinancing of positions or liquidation are likely to be needed. Speculative financing units become dependent upon the order of financial markets and the liquidity supplied. Any disruption in financial markets and in financing processes unfavourably influences the solvency of speculative financing units.

For Ponzi units the present value of cash flows from operations and assets are not sufficient to meet both the interest payments on their debts and all payments due on their maturing liabilities over an extended horizon. Ponzi units must engage in position-making and/or liquidation. However, these alternatives would probably decrease their net worth and solvency. Furthermore, due to the fact that Ponzi units capitalise interest on debts, their equity account decreases and the debt account increases. According to Minsky, for both speculative and Ponzi units the composition of their debt structure is very likely to change with short-term debt financing growing faster relative to long-term debt and equity financing. Note that in this approach, large financial disruptions and increasing interest rates can transform hedge units to speculative units, and speculative units to Ponzi units, thereby undermining the robustness of the financial structure.[11] If leverage increases at a faster rate than income, in response to rising debt and/or interest rates, the payment/income ratio will rise. As leverage increases, the significance of the uninterrupted income flows also upsurges. Therefore, the more units are involved in position-making to meet balance-sheet commitments with portfolio transactions, the more dependent on the meso-macro conditions, the order and stability of financial markets and central bank's intervention they are.

In this framework, Minsky (1970) asserted that the domain of stability of the financial system is smaller the closer the articulation between cash outflows and cash inflows, the smaller the weight of protected assets in portfolios, and the larger the extent to which asset prices reflect both growth expectations and realised past appreciations. In his *Stabilising an Unstable Economy*, Minsky (1986b) proclaimed that the higher the ratio of hedge units, the more robust an economy's financial structure. In contrast, the higher the ratio of speculative and Ponzi units, the more fragile is an economy's financial structure. Seen from a macro-angle, financial stability hinges upon the quality and sustainability of the financial structure of the full employment effective demand, the dynamics of layering and the order and liquidity of financial markets. These forces rule the coherence between cash inflows from income production operations and refinancing and cash outflows embodied in the inherited liability structures. Minsky (1982) noted that if financial developments that go along with economic growth lean towards a higher debt/income ratio of the private sector or a decrease in the stock of liquidity, then the possibility of financial instability and debt deflation increases as growth continues. This possibility increases if the assets protected by the central bank are few and the markets are thin. Under such conditions, the selling out of a position will cause a severe collapse in the asset price inducing a sharp reduction in organisation's net worth, especially if it is over-leveraged. Banks and other financial institutions that hold the liabilities of corporations and households operate as channels that propagate and amplify or dampen episodes of defaults and bankruptcies. A point to stress is that, for Minsky, if rolling over debt is a common characteristic of business financing processes, the solvency of financial organisations is imperative for the income-generating process and hence for the solvency regime of business firms. In addition, if the assets held by financial institutions fail to perform, the cash flows collapse and their risk aversion increases. This then is likely to cause significant macroeconomic implications, as financial institutions would reduce the financing of consumption and investment spending. Most importantly, a fall in effective demand would reduce the income and cash flows for units and, hence, their capability to fulfil debt payments. Unsustainable liability structures would, eventually, negatively affect aggregate demand and the macroeconomy. Therefore, for Minsky, as Tymoigne (2006; 2012) pointed out, financial fragility is an endogenous phenomenon that emerges when income flows fail to maintain the quality of liability structures; and when institutional arrangements do not guarantee refinancing positions.

An important aspect of Minsky's analysis is that financial fragility escalates if the organisations are collateral-based and especially if financial markets are thin. In Minsky's system, the solvency risk and default risk of speculative and Ponzi units that are collateral-based are higher because their refinancing entails balance sheet and portfolio transactions. As Tymoigne (2012) argued, Ponzi units in particular can meet their debt commitments only through refinancing and/or liquidation of asset positions at growing asset prices. Thus, higher value of collateral and asset prices are preconditions for Ponzi units to create the net worth that qualifies financial institutions to refinance their position-making. If asset prices and the value of collaterals plunge, Ponzi units would fail to make net worth and banks might deleverage, decreasing their possibility of refinancing. This then is likely to incentivise the liquidation of loans and of asset positions. Consequently, the balance sheet of Ponzi organisations which are collateral-based contains higher solvency risk. Unsustainable solvency aggravates the uncertainty over the complexity between asset prices, refinancing and debt and payment commitments. This result is even larger if the practically unregulated and highly leveraged shadow banks control a significant segment of the liquidity supplied by the financial system. In contrast, financial stability is more probable to eventuate if there is a significant portion of hedge units, which create income flows from normal operations.

Concluding, MFIH illustrates that financial markets are not self-equilibrating and they do not optimally allocate savings. They are inherently unstable and misallocate liquidity, especially in the money manager stage of capitalism. In contrast with the 'efficient market hypothesis', MFIH entails the necessity of financial and macroeconomic management.

The co-evolution between the financial system and the macro-system

MFIH contextualises how the dynamics of layering and the order and liquidity of financial markets affect units' solvency risk and balance-sheet adjustments. This then influences units' position-making and liquidation. Minsky's (1975a; 1986b) 'two-price systems' exemplifies the financial and macroeconomic dynamics of leverage and liability creation processes.[12] These dynamics demonstrate how the evolution of finance influences the co-evolution among the business, financial end macroeconomic systems. In fact, Minsky's conceptualisation establishes how the evolution of finance disturbs the capacity of the macro-system to attain and secure full employment. Minsky's 'two-price systems' emanate from his endeavour to incorporate Kalecki's conceptualisation of the relation between income distribution and aggregate spending into his Schumpeterian-Keynesian financial structure of liability valuation.

Minsky's first price system is the asset-price system, which is divided into the price of financial assets and the price of real capital assets. Kregel (1992) marked out that the asset-price system contextualises Minsky's interpretation of Keynes's analysis of liquidity preference. Attention is paid to three factors, namely the creation of money and credit, the financial commitments and the expected profits (in the Kalecki's sense) in the long-term. Variations in this price system are hypothesised to cause significant macroeconomic consequences, because they influence the aggregate rate of investment undertaken by firms. Investment is seen as one of the most fundamental components of effective demand and hence it determines the aggregate profit and cash flows realised and distributed among organisations. Minsky presumed that units' positive investment decisions are taken if there is a high state of animal spirit. This presupposition implies that there are optimistic projections of the capitalised value of expected profits that exceeds the supply price of investment output; and, in addition, that the expected difference between cash inflow and cash outflow is adequate to improve the confidence of risk averse businessmen and bankers. The price level of investment output is determined by the institutions that rule the money wage-setting, the interest cost of financing and the expected excess of prices over production cost.

Note that in Minsky's scrutiny of the asset-price system, emphasis is focused on the distribution of carrying risk and insurance among money, financial assets and capital assets. It is hypothesised that if the expected profitability from using capital assets is high, given their insurance, the price of capital assets will be high, hence investment will increase. Profit maximising bankers will look impatiently for new opportunities to endogenously expand the liquidity supplied. Minsky (1990, p. 60) upheld that financial innovations usually loosen unit's external financing constraints, when there exists discrepancies between the price level of capital assets and the price level of investment output. However, the financing of investment increases debt leveraging for both corporations and banks. Initially, an increase in leverage boosts investment, effective demand and profits. But, if leverage is driven by over-optimism, solvency illusions and speculative innovations and practices, then, Minsky claimed that, the inherited debt structure will increase liabilities at a faster rate than investment increases productive capacity and income flows. A higher debt/income ratio and high interest payments shift the distribution of capital income towards, Keynes's, rentiers. This distribution effect reduces entrepreneurial income, liquidity and investment, and, unless compensated by other profit-inducing spending, the aggregate capital income. Argitis (2017) pinpointed that in Minsky's formulation, a fall in aggregate profits evidences that organisations have possibly been engaged in leverage structures that make them incapable of preserving the solvency of their liability structures. This then increases the risk of debt payment commitments not being met and the likelihood of deleveraging. However, deleveraging in business and banking sectors is a propagation mechanism that induces cumulative processes that are likely to transform small monetary and financial shocks into financial crises. For Minsky, this possibility shows the macro-reasoning of examining the aggregate liability structure of organisations. He proposed various financial ratios to detect the solvency risk of units, among them the ratio of business indebtedness to total estimated value of business assets and the ratio of payment commitments on debts to total gross capital income. Under the assumption that these ratios increase, an economy's financial structure is fragile and becomes dependent upon small negative changes in expected profits or increases in interest rates. However, the debt-carrying capacity of any organisation depends not only on expected cash flows, but also on the margins of safety that borrowers and lenders find acceptable.

Profits are a core element in Minsky's macro-vision. According to Minsky (1985–1986, p. 7), profits "are the raw material for the formation of bankers' and businessmen's expectations, that lead to investment and financing conditions, and they furnish funds to financing institutions, which enable them to acquire new issues that finance investment". What is remarkable in his argument is that if, at a given level of investment, actual profits are lower than the expected profits, the margin of safety between unit's expected cash inflows and the cash flows required to validate its debt will increase. This means that less debt than before can be carried by the expected cash inflows. Minsky stressed that a higher solvency risk of a liability structure constrains an organisation's capacity to issue new debt. However, adjustments in banks' and investors' anticipation of a unit's margins of safety affect its market valuation and, therefore, the refinancing of position-making and the materialisation of investment plans. Nevertheless, cash flows and refinancing uncertainty generates insecurity about a unit's competence to endure its leverage structure and to meet debt commitments. Moreover, if cash flows are largely less than cash commitments, firms and their creditors are exposed to the risks of default and liquidation. The default risk hinges upon the quality of a unit's leverage structure and increases when solvency risk rises. Both the solvency and default risks increase uncertainty over investment and effective demand. Besides, Dymski and Pollin (1992) observed that in Minsky's system, investment uncertainty also arises from market risk. If non-financial organisations fail to evaluate precisely the market risk which is related to changes in the asset prices on secondary markets, then the default risk of their portfolio upsurges. Minsky (1970) pointed out the possibility that over-leverage will prompt banks to take on liquidity-decreasing portfolio transformations, accepting low quality liability structures. A hypothetically enormous drop in asset prices would make firms and banks incapable of meeting debt commitments and hence to sustain the quality of their balance sheets. He endorsed that any fall in the price of real capital assets relative to the price level of current output and of money may encourage portfolio changes plummeting new positions in real assets and boosting positions in portfolio and balance-sheet transactions. Nevertheless, this effect would cause a negative impact on the 'real' resource creation processes that generate sustainable income and cash flows, which preserve solvency.

Yet, the market valuation of asset and liability procedures also depends on expectations about variations of the second price system, which is Minsky's output-price system. The latter manifests a unit's cash inflow potentials and portrays the technical conditions of production that are encompassed in the valuation of capital assets; the various costs of production including the labour cost; the market power of an organisation; and its capability to exploit the market power to make higher profits. The state of effective demand is vital as it determines the realised revenues and cash inflows. One of Minsky's most useful observations is that corporations make use of market power to set the mark-up and hence the price level, in a Kaleckian manner. In Minsky's system, as Papadimitriou and Wray (1998) pinpointed, the administration of nominal prices advances the control of corporations over income distribution and nominal cash inflows. In this way corporations can manipulate market expectations regarding their solvency regime and liquidity and default risks.

In this context, Minsky's 'two-price systems' integrate asset values with the value of the insurance and liquidity of money, investments with the relation between asset values and current output prices, profits with investments and debt validations with profits. Stable periods create optimism that rewards borrowers' and lenders' risky behaviour in building liability structures. Unrealised profits and unfulfilled liability commitments increase solvency and default risks, which bring about liquidation and falls in capital and financial asset prices. Uncertainty over the value of banks' liabilities and low margins of safety are a possible source of deleveraging and financial panic. Accordingly, Minsky upheld that booms activate endogenous processes that make financial structures more fragile, especially if they are unregulated, thereby increasing the possibility of Fischer's debt-deflation processes. This is even more likely to happen when governments and central banks do not intervene to prevent speculative and, especially, Ponzi financial processes.

The financial structure of effective demand and the evolution of the macro-system

In Minsky's system, macroeconomic order is a process of capital development that combines full employment with price stability under the presupposition that these effects can be attained and sustained by financial market processes. Following Keynes, Minsky (1975a) made a distinction between growth and full employment. He envisioned a full employment, effective demand as a precondition for economic units to generate income creation and distribution processes and sustainable cash flows to maintain their solvency and position-making at the micro-meso level. Tymoigne (2006) points out that, for Minsky, an under-full employment economic growth, which reflects a state of insufficient demand, induces uncertainty over the cash inflows of units that increase their solvency risk. In contrast, macroeconomic disorder is perceived as a process where insufficient aggregate demand and unemployment render economic units incapable of generating sustainable income and cash flows so as to preserve their solvency and position-making. On the other hand, Minsky envisaged financial order and stability as complex liquidity creation and refinancing processes that sustain the effective demand close to full employment. Yet, this principle ensures units' solvency. In contrast, financial instability is a process through which micro-distress and defaults induced by coordination failures of cash flow and interrupted refinancing processes escalate into a solvency and liquidity crisis at the meso level and into a debt deflation and, possibly, depression at the macro level.

The co-evolution between the financial system and the macro-system becomes more complicated when Minsky integrated households' debt into an economy's financial structure.[13]Minsky (1982) divided household debt financing and cash payment commitments into financing of consumption and financing of ownership of real assets, housing and financial assets. He claimed that household debt financing of consumption is always hedge financing, while financing of asset ownership is Ponzi in nature. The cash flows that validate consumption financing emanate from household's disposable income, which is, for the most part, wages.[14] If actual wage income falls short of that originally anticipated, and under the assumption that other variables that determine disposable income are constant, then this fall can transform a hedge financing into a speculative or Ponzi financing household. An important aspect of Minsky's analysis is that if an increase in consumption spending by households is debt-financed, then the link between household wage income, household consumption and effective demand becomes more complex and uncertain. In addition, it is predisposed to changes in income distribution and to monetary and financial developments. Moreover, income distribution changes at the expense of wages would negatively affect, apart from consumption and saving, household's capacity to meet debt commitments. It is important to underline that for Minsky, the solvency regime of a household is affected by the portion of Ponzi finance in an economy's financial structure. For instance, if a speculative appreciation of asset values takes place, a household might increase its debt/income ratio because of higher market value of collateral. However, household's cash flows from production and distribution of income processes might not be adequate to meet outstanding payment commitments. In such a case, the posture of a household's financing regime will depend on the sustainability of asset prices.

The financial structure of effective demand becomes even more complex after the incorporation of government debt. In his argumentation, Minsky focused on sovereign countries to examine the potential destabilising role of government sector.[15] Government units are conceived to be speculative financing units, which regularly operate by rolling over short-term debt. If the total future expected cash inflows – mainly from taxes net of current expenses – exceed the total future cash payment commitments on the current outstanding debt, there are no solvency and roll over problems. However, high interest rates and high primary deficits can transform speculative government units into Ponzi ones.

This analysis makes apparent that the validation of the total debt for an economy, or for sub-sectors, relies on whether several components of national income are large enough to allow maturing commitments to be fulfilled either out of profits, wages, taxes, etc., or out of refinancing. But refinancing depends on anticipated future cash flows. Therefore, at all times the emerging evidence on the change of major distributive variables must signal anticipated inflows which make refinancing possible. In the case of the business sector, anticipated profits after dividends and taxes are decisive because they are internal funds and cash flows that do or do not validate a debt structure used to finance capital assets. Note that a fall in investments diminishes profits and national income. Furthermore, the validation of debt determines the liability structures which businessmen and bankers accept. In an economy in which there are solvency problems, a potential decline in actual profits from expected levels increases default risk and reduces the quality of leverage. Thus, the expected variations of profits are a significant determinant of the acceptable quality of a liability structure. Minsky (1982) illustrated, in a Kaleckian demand-driven profit framework, various factors to explain the variation and stability of business profits and so their stabilising/destabilising effects on the financial structure. In this framework, the profit generating processes include investment, budget deficit, exports, imports, savings out of wage income, and consumption out of profits income. The various Kalecki's profit creation processes indicate that the acceptable quality of a debt financing of demand relies on endogenous (structural) and exogenous (policy and institutional) variables that stabilise profits.

Minsky (1982, pp. 41–44) discussed the relation between debt and income within several institutional structures to illustrate the financial and macroeconomic interconnectedness. The starting place is a closed economy with inherited debt and a small government. In such an economy the capacity of debtors to validate their debt structure depends on expectations that future investment will be high enough, so that future profits and cash flows will be large enough for the new debts to be repaid or refinanced, given acceptable margins of safety. Minsky's most important argument was that as the financing of new investment is governed by an economy's financial and banking structures, speculative financial innovations might alter the financing terms eventually inducing fluctuations in investment, in profit expectations and in the validation of debts. Minsky remarked that such an economy will tend to be cyclically unstable, because the liability structures cannot be sustained if total investment failed to generate the required profits and income flows; and also because of the subjective nature of expectations about the future course of investment and effective demand. Accordingly, a stable growth with full employment and financial stability is not a likely outcome in an institutional structure in which private investment and debt-financed ownership of capital assets are market determined. The probability is even lower under the hypothesis that unregulated and speculative financial innovations grow.

Minsky initially visualised the simple Kalecki's profit equation to mark out the association between financial fragility and the expected volatility of private investment. After that he incorporated into his analysis the abovementioned institutional, structural and policy determinants of gross profits. He asserted that, in an economy with a big government, an increase in the government deficit can counterbalance the negative effect of declining investment on profits. This then will reduce the risk premium and the rate at which firms and financial institutions fail to fulfil their liability obligations. Otherwise, the weight of speculative and Ponzi finance in the financial structure will increase activating financial fragility. Therefore, a rising government deficit tends to increase profits and the quality of liability structures, thus reducing the likelihood of financial structure becoming speculative or Ponzi. It is essential to point out that this stabilising effect of a big government might also have destabilising implications. Minsky laid emphasis on the possibility that borrowers and lenders increase their indebtedness, when they identify a decline in the downward pressure on profits. In addition, the stabilisation of aggregate profits by government deficits might activate inflationary consequences. In particular, Minsky supposed that sustained and rising deficits and profits could induce inflation. As argued in detail in the next chapter, this outcome is very possible if public spending is not targeted to promote full employment.

In the case of an open economy with a big government, a favourable balance of trade further sustains and increases profits. Besides, higher profits might advance the capacity of investors to increase their leverage because higher profits advantage their solvency and margins of safety. However, Minsky has cast doubt upon the dependency of domestic profits on large balance of trade surpluses, because of their vulnerability to negative external conditions. A fall in the trade surplus – or an increase in the trade deficit – will worsen domestic profits and the quality of the financial structure, especially if government is small.

Conclusions

Minsky's fundamental contribution to evolutionary macroeconomics is that debt-driven market economies evolve through processes of creation and destruction in financial markets that bring about fragility, instability and debt deflation instead of coherence, full employment and steady growth. Coherence prevails when coordination between cash inflows and cash outflows sustains unit's solvency and capacity to cover new lines of liquidity, so as to successfully meet the commitments derived by evolving liability structures. However,

Keynes's fundamental uncertainty and endogenous financial processes make the coordination between cash inflow and cash outflow implausible. This then increases the reliance of organisations on refinancing sources and/or asset liquidation in order to fulfil debt payments.

If financial markets are thin, the possibility of financial and non-financial economic units becoming insolvent and illiquid upsurges. Over-leverage and unsustainable cash flows cause powerful repercussions on the balance sheet of business and banks and on income creation processes. Minsky's units desire to hold cash cushions to avoid insolvency, liquidity crunches and default risk. Nevertheless, banks' solvency illusions and risky financial innovations induce over-leverage and possibly large-scale defaults, deleverage and debt deflation.

MFIH is an evolutionary interpretation of Keynes's *General Theory*, which contextualises the key role of financial linkages, institutions and markets into a financial macro-evolutionary theorisation. This theorisation incorporates continuous and cumulative changes in financial relations and structures to illustrate the susceptibility of capitalist economies to financial fragility and instability. Emphasis is given to how evolutionary finance affects the volatility of private investment and the speculative behaviour of organisations in a euphoric economy. Minsky held that unregulated financial processes parasitise the symbiosis between financial system and macro-system. His 'two-price systems' operate as an institutional blender which reveals that the macro-system is predisposed to cycles of over-leverage and deleverage, unsustainable liability structures and debt deflation.

Closing, for Minsky, there is a permanent problem of insufficient demand in a capitalist economy. This problem is not due to wages, price or interest rate rigidities. Financial structures and institutions are the probable forces that make the failure of investment and effective demand an endogenous phenomenon. Nevertheless, the endogenous explosive forces could be controlled by institutional and policy adaptation targeting the coordination failures of cash flows and the protection of asset values for portfolios starving for safety, liquidity and solvency. As it will be argued in the next chapter, if the break in the boom causes financial instability, debt deflation and depression or a non-traumatic recession will depend upon the order and liquidity of financial markets, the size of the government sector, and the discount window and lender-of-last-resort actions by the central bank.

Notes

1   A large number of theoretical and empirical articles and books about Minsky's method, theory and policy proposals have been published (see e.g. Fazzari and Papadimitriou, 1992; Dymski and Pollin, 1994; Bellofiore and Ferri, 2001; Papadimitriou and Wray, 1997; 1998; 2010; Tavasci and Toporowski, 2010; Whalen, 2011; Tymoigne and Wray, 2014; Wray, 2016).

2   I use the term micro-meso-macro in a taxonomic sense, and not in an ontological sense describing rules and populations, as it is used by evolutionary economists (see e.g. Dopfer, 2001; 2005; 2012; Dopfer et al., 2004; Dopfer and Potts, 2008; Foster, 2011).

3 As analysed in the text, in Minsky's system, units' position-making is the process of making spending and financing decisions and portfolio transactions to meet balance-sheet commitments.

4 See e.g. Nelson and Winter (1982), Nelson (1995), Foster (2000), Fagerberg (2003), Dopfer (2005; 2012).

5 Minsky (1977a, p. 141) argued that "Wall Street will serve as the label for the institutions and usages that generate and allocate the finance for investment and for positions in the inherited stock of capital assets. In our economy the behaviour of Wall Street is a determinant of the pace and direction of investment. A model of the economy from the perspective of Wall Street differs from the standard model of economic theory in that it first sees a network of financial interrelations and cash flows and then a production and distribution mechanism. A wall Street paradigm is a better starting point for theorising about our type of economy than the barter paradigm of conventional theory".

6 Minsky (1986a, p. 118) argued that Keynes's "asset pricing model and the view of banking by which cash flaws that validate contracts destroy money even as new financing creates money, implies that nominal values matter to agents that own, finance and create capital assets. One cannot legitimately use production functions and preference systems over real variables to determining anything of significance in a capitalist economy with a modern banking system". In addition, he emphasised that "a further implication of the denial of the axiom of reals is that Walras and Keynes are like oil and water; they don't mix".

7 Throughout his writings, Minsky maintained that there are differences among capitalist economies due to the institutional evolution of their financial systems. He used the slogan '57 varieties of capitalism'. He claimed that the US capitalism has institutionally evolved through five financial stages of development, namely, commercial capitalism, industrial capitalism, financial capitalism, managerial and welfare state capitalism and money manager capitalism (see e.g. Minsky 1986a; 1992a; 1996).

8 Minsky's mental models are different from the 'true' model that is presumed by conventional equilibrium macroeconomics to guide the formation of rational expectations and choices, which constitute a precondition for equilibrium. For Minsky, agents can make systematic wrong decisions, not because of bounded rationality or of asymmetric information, but because of Keynes's fundamental uncertainty. Minsky (1996, p. 359) asserted that "the uncertainty that permeates the economics of Keynes and the economics of bounded rationality is due to the unsureness about the validity of the model of the economy that enters in the decision process".

9 For most households and non-financial business firms the principal source of cash is their current income. Wages and salaries are the major liquidity source for households and realised sales of output are the major liquidity source for non-financial institutions. For banks and other financial institutions the usual cash inflows are derived from their financial asset structure.

10 Minsky's argument includes all economic units, which could be a business firm, household, financial institution, or a government unit.

11 Minsky (1995a) argued that when small shocks are absorbed without much difficulty, then the financial structure is robust; when small shocks cause large effects and the financial system is incapable of returning back to stability, then the financial structure is fragile.

12 It is worthy to pinpoint Minsky's comment that the absence of attention, from conventional Keynesian economists, to his 'two-price systems' is due to their belief that fine-tuning macroeconomic policy can stabilise the capitalist economies (see e. g. Ferri and Minsky, 1989). In contrast, Minsky used his 'two-price systems' to place emphasis on economy's fragile financial structure and to the negotiations and deals

among households, businessmen, bankers and the government as an everyday practice in order to dispute the stabilising effectiveness of fine-tuning.

13 It is significant to note that Minsky laid emphasis mostly on the business and banking sectors to illustrate the endogenous destabilising financing and funding processes
of private investment. However, as household debt and government debt have
astonishingly increased, especially in the current financialisation era, their solvency,
debt dynamics and cash flows have indisputably increased their weight in the analysis of financial macroeconomic instability and order. As a result, Minsky's analysis
of these issues is significant.

14 In a broader definition household's income includes transfer receipts/payments,
dividend and interest income.

15 For non-sovereign countries, as Bell (2003), Wray (2003), Sardoni and Wray (2006),
Kelton and Wray (2009) and Argitis and Nikolaidi (2014) argued, the solvency
posture of the government sector is significant for an economy's financial fragility,
because these countries cannot finance their expenditures and debt obligations by
issuing their own currency. Their margin of safety and perceived credit risk of
government bonds in the financial markets are estimated by the excess of the
expected government revenues over the sum of the expected primary expenditures.
If the credit risk is conceived to be high, then the refinancing of government
expenditures and debt payments can be disrupted, inducing downward pressures on
aggregate demand and on economic growth. Ferrari-Filho et al. (2010) and Argitis
and Nikolaidi (2014) have proposed and estimated Minskian fragility ratios for the
government sector.

4   Minsky's institutional stabilisers and endogenous capitalist instability

Introduction

For Minsky, a practical program of reforms and interventions should recognise that economic policy must permanently adapt to speculative and Ponzi leverage along with liability creation processes. The financial and macroeconomic systems constantly evolve, so stability and order cannot be permanently assured. When debt increases faster than income and the macroeconomy fails to attain conditions of full employment, then financial fragility and instability will happen as a result of a snowball of defaults and bankruptcies. If speculative and Ponzi finance that 'naturally' result from market processes are not appropriately contained, they will ultimately induce debt deflation and depression.

As analysed in detail below, Minsky fully adopted the thrust of Keynes's political economy in relation to the inherently unstable nature of the rentier model of capitalism. Keynes's vision led Minsky to dispute the self-regulated financial markets illusion and fine-tuning illusion of the habitual financial and macroeconomic theories. In his macro-vision, the free market ideology is incompatible with the institutional structure of modern debt-driven market economies. Minsky conceptualised a system of institutional ceilings and floors to stabilise profits, asset prices and the credibility of borrowers' and lenders' margins of safety so as to constrain financial instability. His policy propositions were institution-specific and aimed at creating a more stable, efficient and humane form of capitalism.

Keynes's pragmatism and Minsky's political economy

Minsky's conceptualisation of economic policy grew out of his conviction that Keynes's political economy[1] was the appropriate framework to contemplate the necessary policies and reforms to advance an institutionally successful variant of capitalism.[2] As I have argued elsewhere (Argitis, 2008–2009, pp. 250–251), Keynes endorsed that classical economics was inadequate to resolve the crucial problems that capitalist economies faced in the inter-war period, mainly unemployment. Keynes transformed himself from a classical into an anticlassical monetarist theorist because of the practical implications of classical economics, which were fundamentally laissez-faire biased; and the anti-pragmatism of the classical theory of interest, which relegates the 'fundamentals' of a monetary production economy. The economic, social and political developments in the 1920s led Keynes to progress towards anti-laissez-faire policy principles. It must be emphasised that this development in Keynes's political philosophy was profoundly related to the growth of his monetary thought. The latter was fully crystallised in *The General Theory of Employment, Interest and Money* (1936), where Keynes particularised the monetary and financial structures of capitalist economies and scrutinised the economic, social and political possibilities of full employment.

In the *A Tract on Monetary Reform* (1923), Keynes credited all major ills of capitalism (e.g. unemployment, insecurity, uncertainty, speculation) to monetary instability and called attention to the distributional effects of inflation and deflation on rentiers and the active and constructive entrepreneur class of capitalists. In the *Poverty in Plenty: Is the Economic System Self-Adjusting?* (1934), Keynes included himself among the 'heretics' who have no doubt that the capitalist economic system is not self-adjusting because of the functioning of the monetary and financial systems. Keynes (1934, p. 389) remarked that

> there is, I am convinced, a fatal flaw in that part of the orthodox reasoning which deals with the theory of what determines the level of effective demand and the volume of aggregate employment; the flaw being largely due to the failure of the classical doctrine to develop a satisfactory theory of the rate of interest.

By rebutting the classical theory of interest[3] and gradually replacing it with his monetary theory of interest, Keynes was on the way to build the monetary and financial foundations of his social philosophy, which as, Dillard (1946, p. 122) remarks, "may be characterised as an attack on financial capitalism and a defence of industrial capitalism".

Minsky (1975a) claimed that Keynes's political economy draws the institutional prerequisites for a capitalist economy to succeed the triad of economic efficiency, social justice and individual liberty. In his viewpoint, Keynes correlated this triad with the volume of investment and interventions in income distribution that advance employment and economic efficiency. Minsky's emphasis was upon Keynes's successful variant of capitalism, which appears the one that can guarantee the aforementioned triad. But, this is implausible to happen in monetary production economies, because of the special properties of money. This is the wisdom of *The General Theory of Employment, Interest and Money* where Keynes structured his principle of effective demand on the reality of finance and interest. In Keynes's vision, the special nature of money functions as a structural barrier to full employment. The properties of money and the reality of the complex and speculative financial markets, combined with uncertainty, induce investors to prefer liquidity to real assets. Keynes's bias against rentier capitalism is indicated by his underlying socio-economic reforms that encourage employment and industrial entrepreneurship as essential preconditions for a more efficient and humane variant of capitalism. In his socio-political vision, a presupposition for the endurance of entrepreneurial capitalism is the evaporation of rentier capitalism.[4] This conception attributes to Keynes's political economy a dualism between finance and industry (Dillard, 1946; 1948). Argitis (2008–2009) marked out that Keynes conceptualised the 'euthanasia' of rentiers' income as the primary target of macroeconomic policy so as to increase the propensity to consume, the inducement to invest and economic efficiency.

Minsky (1975a) appreciated Keynes's political economy and social philosophy and especially his call for the 'euthanasia' of rentiers in order to remove the monetary impediments to a more equal distribution of income and to full employment. However, Minsky's pro-pragmatism bias enabled him to think more practical about the institutional prerequisites of Keynes's successful and full employment variant of capitalism. He entirely endorsed Keynes's insight that capitalism is unable to manage itself. In this regard, Minsky (1986b) introduced the concept of 'conditional coherence' of the Wall Street capitalist model, which becomes dependent upon certain institutions. Ferri and Minsky (1991, p. 4) proclaimed that "institutions and interventions thwart the instability breeding dynamics that are natural to market economies by interrupting the endogenous process and starting the economy again with non-market determined values as initial conditions". Furthermore, Minsky et al. (1994, p. 2) stated that "to contain the evils that market systems can inflict, capitalist economies developed sets of institutions and authorities, which can be characterised as the equivalent of circuit breakers". Besides, Ferri and Minsky (1991, p. 20) identified that "in a world where the internal dynamics imply instability, a semblance of stability can be achieved or sustained by introducing conventions, constraints and interventions into the environment". Consequently, Minsky envisioned institutions and interventions not as barriers to full employment equilibrium,[5] but as stabilising vehicles to bring about financial stability and to attain full employment with price stability. His main concern was to identify the institutions and the processes that destabilise the market economies and to manifest institutions and policies that stabilise them. And in this endeavour he drew particular attention to endogenous speculative and Ponzi financial structures and the enduring liquidity, solvency and asset valuation problems of the business and banking sectors.

A point to underline is that Minsky's elaboration of Keynes's political economy qualified him to contemplate the role of declining private investment in the failure of effective demand to achieve full employment. Minsky added financial sophistication to this principle. He considered the role of private investment via his solvency analysis of the cash flow dynamics at micro-meso levels that rule the financial structure of effective demand. As explained in the previous chapter, for Minsky, investment is more volatile than the other components of aggregate demand because of the investor's subjective evaluations of solvency risk, revisions of rules of thumb and variations in the perceived lender's and borrower's risk and margins of safety. In this vein, Minsky (1979, p. 96) argued that "the greater the proportion of private investment in Gross National Income and the greater the weight of speculative and Ponzi finance in the totality of financial relations the more unstable the economy". This conception relies on MFIH (Minsky's 'financial instability hypothesis') and the premise that a private sector's investment boom is 'naturally' correlated with more speculative and Ponzi solvency structures. Therefore, an investment boom is destabilising, because it erodes the quality of an economy's financial structure.

Furthermore, Minsky asserted that these destabilising effects augment if the capital intensity of investment upsurges. Throughout his writings, he decidedly hypothesised that the greater are the investment bias and the capital intensity bias of economic policy, the higher an economy's inefficiency and instability. Accordingly, Minsky's approach to economic policy reflects upon the pre-dominated and legislated institutional structure that carries a pro-investment bias and an anti-employment bias. The prevailing institutional reality is, to a significant degree, accountable for the unemployment, instability, inefficiency and inequality in market economies. So, for Minsky, an essential program of institutional reforms needs to target the elimination of the pro-investment bias and the anti-employment bias of economic policy. In this way interventions will minimise the likelihood of financial instability and underpin macro-economic coherence. These insights configure Minsky's political economy, which is biased towards a variety of capitalism in which Keynes's rentiers are not eventually euthanised, but in which a regulated financial system works for capital development and the full employment of labour.

A first point to stress is that a significant constituent of Minsky's political economy is his 'two-price systems'. The latter enabled Minsky (1987b) to con-ceptualise the building blocks of a macroeconomic safety net to accomplish full employment,[6] stability, efficiency and equality. A second point to underline is that this safety net should be evolutionary and must continuously adapt to the growing financial and macroeconomic environment. In the following passage Minsky (1986b, p. 7) exemplified his evolutionary thinking. He observed that

> economic systems are not natural systems. An economy is a social organi-sation created either through legislation or by an evolutionary process of invention and innovation. Policy can change both the details and the overall character of the economy, and the shaping of economic policy involves both a definition of goals and an awareness that actual and eco-nomic processes depend on economic and social institutions.

Minsky proclaimed that a successful safety net must integrate and coordinate the institutions of Big Government and Big Bank. The institution of Big Government should function, through fiscal policy interventions, as an expen-diture system for the private sector. This expenditure system must stabilise and increase current output prices so as to balance a fall in profit flows before pri-vate investment falls; and, in addition, to allocate directly resources towards the activation of employment and resource-creation practices. On the other hand, the institution of Bing Bank must act as a stabiliser in the financial markets. It must come in to sustain the quality of balance sheets by preventing falls in the prices of capital and financial assets relative to current output prices. In this context, it becomes apparent that fiscal and monetary policies are taken, by

Minsky, to be procedures that would continuously adjust to incessant financial and macroeconomic changes. Organisations make value judgments in calendar time that involve re-evaluations of various position-making. The continuous adaptation of policy institutions is therefore essential so as to be able to continuously monitor the quality of the financial structure of effective demand.

Fiscal policy: an institutional financial macroeconomic stabiliser

Minsky's view on the appropriate role of government in market economies hinges upon Keynes's conception of an effective demand gap in the private-enterprise economy and the need for a counter-cyclical government budget. MFIH contextualises Keynes's philosophy and, in addition, places profits at the epicentre of stabilisation policy. As I noted previously, in Minsky's system, profits must be stabilised because their downside variability is very likely to cause coordination failures of cash flows and insolvency. The latter increases the incapability of economic units to validate their inherited debt and past investment decisions. According to Minsky (1986b, p. 24), government deficit causes three stabilising effects: an income and employment effect, which emanates from the influence that the government spending has on the aggregate effective demand; the budget effect, which results from the influence of government deficit on the aggregate profits and cash flows of the non-government sectors. Minsky emphasised that these cash flows improve organisations debt-carrying capacity and margins of safety; and the portfolio effect that reflects the impact that government debt has on the composition of private portfolios, which continuously adjust to the evolving balance between protected and unprotected assets. He hypothesised that an increase in government deficit contains downward pressures on financial and capital asset prices preserving the quality of balance sheets, while an increase in government debt advances the weight of protected assets in private portfolios.

More specifically, Minsky envisaged government deficit as an institution that establishes ceilings and floors that constrain the endogenous instability of market economies. In his vision, the financial structure of a government-spending-led growth is more robust than is the financial structure of a private-sector-spending-led growth. The logic of his argument is that if fiscal policy aims to activate incentives to boost private investments financed through higher levels of leverage, it might eventually increase financial fragility and instability. Besides, Minsky claimed that a fiscal policy that aims at the creation of conditions favourable to private investment might eventually cause inflation. The reason is that wages and prices are likely to increase before a sufficient quantity of jobs is created and output is produced and supplied.

Minsky believed deeply in the possibility that a big government's wrong stabilisation policy may be destabilising. For Minsky (1979), the current fiscal system seeks to sustain stability by managing aggregate demand through transfers, including interest on public debt. In his viewpoint, such a system is not a resource-creation process that simultaneously increases aggregate demand and supply. It creates demand and leaves the creation of supply to market forces. This macro-imbalance might cause inflationary tendencies and expectations. In this regard, Minsky (2013) commented on the possibility of increasing inequality due to a fall real wage. The likelihood of an economy experiencing a combination of a fragile and unsustainable growth, unemployment and inequality qualified Minsky to think deeper about the structure and the effectiveness of government spending. One of his most useful policy observations, as analysed in detail below, was that a big government must directly target the creation of jobs for particular unemployed groups. He proposed the restructure of public expenditures and the creation of a fiscal system that would aim to maintain stability by job creation in a manner that is not inflationary. This conception capacitated Minsky, as Tcherneva (2011; 2013) has pointed out, to cast doubt upon the habitual Keynesian call for a general increase of the size of the undirected government spending.

Moreover, Minsky focused his attention on the value of fiscal multiplier. He presumed that if the multiplier is high, it may augment the stabilising effect of government spending on sales and profits. Nevertheless, Minsky was concerned about the possibility of a private investment-led expansion increasing tax revenues faster than private sector income. This imbalance of cash flows will tend to move government budget towards surplus and the private sector balance towards deficit. But, deficit units are liable to solvency risk and default risk. This led Minsky (1979, p. 3) to proclaim that although a big government is essential for financial stability, "too big government, or a big government that does the 'wrong' things, or impacts on markets in particular ways, may abet economic turbulence in a financially fragile environment". In this regard, Minsky was, indeed, concerned about the issue of how big a big government should be. In principle, Minsky argued, the size of government deficit must be big enough to offset swings in private investment and in aggregate effective demand so as to stabilise total profits and cash flows. This denotes that government primary expenditures must be equal, if not larger than, to private investment.

However, as Wray (2018) marked out, Minsky accentuated that a government must run surpluses if the economy approaches full employment, in order to avoid inflationary expectations that will increase the interest rates. For Minsky, higher interest rates might cause a vicious cycle of larger deficits and higher inflation and interest rates that will destabilise the monetary and financial systems. Furthermore, he claimed that large deficits stabilise profits, which, however, may induce higher levels of leverage. In such a case, the possibility of financial fragility will increase, if the creation of liabilities by organisations exceeds the prospective profit streams. On these grounds, Minsky was attentive to a fiscal policy that has become too biased towards deficits. In addition, he was concerned about the solvency risk of public debt. Minsky (1979) initially assumed that the liabilities created by government deficits would enhance financial stability because sovereign bonds are safe and risk free. He further argued that, in principle, the reason for a government to run a balanced budget is to create positive expectations about its capability to run surpluses to validate its debt so as to be valuable for investors. Nevertheless, as Wray (2018) remarked, Minsky worried that if budget is biased towards taxes, transfers, interest payments and other categories of inefficient spending, then its ability to perform its stabilising role diminishes.

However, the fear of an ineffective fiscal policy led Minsky to draw special attention to the balance-sheet effect of government's deficit and debt. He maintained that if a big government runs a surplus or a deficit, it absorbs or creates financial assets acquired by the other sectors and in particular by banks and financial institutions. In most of his writings, he asserted a given marketability of government's debt guaranteed by the central bank. In fact, he implicitly hypothesised that the government sector would always be liquid and capable of meeting its liabilities. Insofar as firms, financial institutions and households are capable of acquiring safe and free of default-risk government assets, they improve their liquidity and capacity to manage solvency risk. This positive balance-sheet effect of government debt reduces the default risk of economic units and the market risk. Besides, Minsky claimed that higher and secure government assets increase the value and quality of private portfolios' collateral. This then advances the refinancing conditions for private debtors. It is worth noting that he also emphasised that a higher public debt counterbalances a fall in private business debt in portfolios held by banks, preventing decreases in their demand and time deposits. Thus, banks and other financial institutions get hold of public debt so as to be liquid and to avoid reductions in their assets and liabilities. In contrast, a small government debt cannot induce the abovementioned significant stabilisation effects, especially during recessions, because the outstanding public debt would not be sizable in private portfolios.

Minsky was also concerned about the increasing use of government debt in private portfolios. The reason was that this portfolio effect might induce destabilising monetary developments that influence the effectiveness of central banking. As discussed in detail below, for Minsky, open market operations to accommodate the trade of sovereign bonds, institutionalise market valuations as a disciplinary mechanism for banks' risky innovations and practices. But, for Minsky, an open market operation central banking is unable to use discretionary power to control individual banks. For this to happen, a central bank should provide reserves at the discount window directly to banks and financial institutions, after having first evaluated the quality of their collateral, balance sheets and solvency risk. The concentration of money creation on the marketability of government debt increases market risk. In addition, Minsky considered, as Wray (2018) argued, a large stock of government debt as a reason of higher interest payments that probably reduce government's capability to run counter-cyclical surpluses in a boom.

Another aspect of Minsky's analysis of government's solvency risk is his assertion that sovereign governments are normally speculative financing units. A speculative government can repay its interest without resorting to new borrowing. However, its primary surplus is not enough to cover the principal repayment (Argitis and Nikolaidi, 2014). They usually operate by rolling over short-term debt and hence by orderly refinancing the validation of their debt commitments by some combination of new borrowing and taxation. As noted in the previous chapter, as long as economic growth ensures that the total future expected public revenue exceeds the total future cash payment commitments on the current outstanding debt, refinancing is possible. Rollover problems arise only if government's finance regime becomes Ponzi that is the primary surplus cannot cover interest payments. However, the more a government remains in a Ponzi solvency regime, the more difficult it is to improve its liquidity position. Higher interest rates increase for a Ponzi government the cost of carrying short-term debt relative to its primary surplus. This, in turn, deteriorates the quality of government's balance sheet and increases the possibility of a government losing access to private financial markets to refinance its maturing debt. Under the assumption of monetary sovereignty, Minsky claimed that a speculative government normally has the funds required to service its debt payments. He emphasised that even a Ponzi government, which is incapable of raising taxes adequately to cover its spending on current operations plus interest on debt, faces no default risk, since it can print money to pay interest. In this regard, Minsky argued that the creditworthiness of a government depends on its organisational capacity to manage taxes and spending in order to create a budget surplus under attainable financial and macroeconomic circumstances. If the government budget turns into surplus as a result of high growth and inflation rates and into deficit due to lower private investment and growth rates, then the institution of Big Government becomes an effective stabiliser of income and cash flows. In such a case, government intervention decreases the likelihood of financial instability and debt-deflation. As long as corporate and household income and cash flows are sustained, due to the effect of government deficit on aggregate demand and profits, the private sector's debt will be validated.

But, according to Minsky (1992b, p. 12)

> government macroeconomic responsibilities depend upon the acceptance of government debt in the market. The funds to validate government debt are derived from taxes, just as the funds that validate private liabilities are derived from profits. The need to protect the public credit is a corollary of the recognition that a capitalist economy is inherently unstable and that the prevention of the disaster of a great depression ultimately depends upon the proper exercise of the public credit.

Seeing Minsky's view from another angle, the sustainability of a government's solvency is preserved by the creation of a taxation system that would keep the government deficit from increasing considerably faster than the government's ability to collect taxes. This principle assures government's solvency. However, Minsky (1986b) noted that public revenues are unable to constantly increase through higher taxation. He was fully aware that taxes induce negative allocation, distribution and macroeconomic effects. In addition, he maintained that higher taxes increase the production cost and cause inflationary pressures and expectations. For this reason, Minsky argued that a government's major responsibility is to fight tax avoidance and evasion and to increase revenues from value-added tax.

At this point, it is worth noting that Minsky (1995b) condemned the balanced budget principle as a time bomb that would begin a financial disaster. He proclaimed that a permanent ceiling to government debt is inharmonious with the stability of the monetary and banking systems. A permanent balance budget cannot contain the repercussions of a fall in aggregate demand on profits, and, in addition, it might make the government's guarantee of deposits worthless. These effects, in combination with the fact that the government debt is the key asset that conforms to the portfolios of risk-adverse units, increase the solvency and market risks. It is important to delineate that deposit insurance has a critical role in Minsky's conceptualisation of the structure of government intervention. Minsky and Campbell (1988) claimed that as non-performing assets and loans increase, deposit insurance from a public agency could compensate for pressures and the systemic risk of the negative net worth of insolvent and failed banks, preventing a wide-ranging run on banks and a credit crunch. Deposit insurance is an effective barrier to debt-deflation and stimulator of stable growth. Its effectiveness relies on the solvency risk of a government and its commitment to accommodate the required liquidity assuring that the deposit liabilities will pay off in full. Minsky (1992b, p. 7) noted that "deposit insurance was never insurance, it was always a pledge of the full faith and credit of the government". Minsky proposed the coverage of deposit insurance to be principally restricted to household size deposits.

In conclusion, Minsky envisaged a targeted fiscal policy that would retain disorderly cyclical forces within bounds, thereby preventing great depressions. Government must be sufficiently big in order to offset through deficit spending any potential fall in private demand. In this way, it will stabilise aggregate profits and organisations' capacity to validate their debt. In order to prevent a solvency and liquidity crisis, government deficit must increase on every occasion the other profit generating mechanisms of a market economy tend to fail to create profit potentials. On the other hand, government surplus must counterbalance the effects of high private demand on inflation. Nevertheless, Minsky designated full employment as the overriding and humane objective of stabilisation policy.

The employer of last resort

The previous discussion shows that for Minsky a big government does not automatically entail that any structure of government spending, taxes, and regulation is effective and socially desirable. As a result, Minsky's analysis of fiscal policy was not concentrated entirely on the size of government deficit; he paid particular attention to the quality and the structure of government spending. He approved that the success of fiscal policy depends on the effectiveness of fiscal measures to reinforce financial macroeconomic coherence. As mentioned, Minsky acknowledged that there are no endogenous processes in market economies that could eradicate involuntary unemployment and poverty. Minsky (2013) was particularly concerned about poverty, which, in his viewpoint, is a matter of unequal income distribution. He proclaimed that conventional anti-poverty strategies were fundamentally flawed, because they focus on how to activate supply-side retraining and re-educating programs to change people[7] and not on how to directly create jobs and income flows to reduce poverty. He endorsed Keynes's principle of effective demand and upheld that the origin of the abovementioned systemic malfunctions is that firms use employment to produce only the quantity of goods they expect to sell. Hence, actual employment is implausible to correspond to full employment. Nonetheless, Minsky (2013) condemned the prevailing fiscal strategy that subsidising demand as a means of achieving full employment. In his view, this fiscal strategy is destabilising because it generates inflationary and distribution changes without creating sustainable conditions to attain full employment. In addition, Wray (2016) remarked that this strategy, by promoting a private investment and transfers-driven growth, activates unstable endogenous financial processes, because part of the private investment would be financed by higher leverage.

In addition, for Minsky (2013), the eradication of income inequality and poverty cannot be counted on inflationary welfare programs that redistribute income from those who work to those who don't. What is even more interesting is that for Minsky, as Wray (2007b) pinpointed, economic policy cannot rely on altruism. The worker and the taxpayer do not anticipate any benefit from welfare programs. Moreover, the structure of benefit-dependent social groups does not lean towards the enhancement of democracy. In this regard, Minsky (2013) proclaimed that employment creation and poverty elimination will have to hinge on an alternative fiscal strategy that directly targets the creation of jobs for the involuntary unemployed. In particular, for Minsky, the policy problem of modern market economies is the institutionalisation of a macro-policy that will fully entail the possibility of achieving tight full employment with price stability in contemporary debt-driven capitalist economies. Note that Minsky claimed that inflationary tendencies and expectations are a barrier to full employment. In his perspective, the realisation of full employment with price stability is critical for governments to transcend the constraints imposed by the deregulated global financial markets on inflationary policy-making.[8] In this way, a government can effectively cope with inequality, poverty and insecurity. According to Minsky, the advantage of job creation fiscal programs is that they materialise a fiscal strategy for full employment that is not inflationary, while it advances employment and equality that will help to promote financial stability and macroeconomic coherence. Minsky's rationale is that job creation programs are not a pure demand-led policy. These programs create supply-side possibilities that will run up against inflationary tendencies and expectations. In addition, note that in the context of MFIH, a full employment macro-system is a prerequisite for financial stability and order.

In this manner, Minsky advocated the institutionalisation of 'employer of last resort' (hereafter ELR) programs pinpointing their capacity potentials for developing a coherent strategy for achieving financial macroeconomic stability and poverty elimination. It is important to stress that Minsky, apart from the ELR strategy, placed emphasis on the encouragement of employment intensive productive processes as well as on taxation and corporate reforms that will target the promotion of capital saving structures of production. It should also be designated that Minsky perceived fiscal policy as a part of a broader developmental strategy. The latter should encompass financial and banking reforms that eradicate the bias of economy policy-making towards private investment.

In his *Stabilising and Unstable Economy*, Minsky (1986b) outlined a sharpened version of his ELR application, which hinges upon government's capacity to offer an infinitely elastic demand for unskilled labour.[9] The essence of Minsky's strategy is that a national government should stand ready to make, at a living wage, a job available to anyone who is able to work, wants to work, but is unable to find a job in market processes. It must be emphasised that an ELR program does not replace public-sector jobs. It aims at providing a job guarantee to anyone legally entitled to work not through market forces, but through government spending (Wray, 1998). A significant parameter of an ELR strategy is that the jobs offered usually pay the legislated minimum wage, which does not depend upon long-term and short-term profit expectations of business. In this context, it is hypothesised that the ELR wage does not induce inflationary pressures in the boom, but it does prevent deflationary pressures in a bust. The adherents of the ELR strategy emphasise that during a boom private employers could hire workers from the ELR pool at a better wage, while in recession the unemployed workers can work at the ELR minimum wage. In this way, the ELR sets a floor to the fall of wages just as central banks' lender-of-last-resort function sets a floor to asset prices. Consequently, the ELR operates as an institutional stabiliser of aggregate disposable income and consumption spending. Note that Minsky visualised consumption as the most stable part of aggregate demand if it is financed out of income rather than debt. For that reason, Minsky supported wages and incomes policy at the bottom of the income distribution, which promotes consumption rather than investment. Furthermore, Wray (2016, p. 35) notified that "Minsky argued that a legislated minimum wage is 'effective' only with an 'employer of last resort' for otherwise the true minimum wage is zero for all those who cannot find a job". Therefore, an ELR program indeed strengthens the institutional role of minimum wage in operating as a benchmark price for labour.[10] As a result, the private sector's jobs that might pay a wage below the ELR minimum wage would normally disappear. By supporting full employment, the ELR strategy might encourage workers in the private sector to claim higher wages.[11]

In the fiscal realm, government spending will move counter cyclically stabilising an economy as ELR spending increases in recession and falls in expansion. Consequently, an ELR full employment program cannot cause demand-pull inflation, since it is designed to ensure that the budget deficit will rise only to the point that all involuntary unemployment is eliminated. When there are workers unwilling to accept ELR jobs and wage rate, government expenditures will not increase. As a result, an ELR program secures that aggregate demand will not boost beyond the full employment level evoking demand-pull inflation. This argument enabled Minsky to suggest a restructuring of government expenditure away from welfare and military spending, which increases aggregate demand without increasing production, towards public infrastructure and job creation that increases both aggregate demand and supply. A final point to stress is that the ELR spending will not necessarily create budget deficits. Given an economy's fiscal multiplier, the rise in GDP, which results from an ELR program, might generate public revenues that are likely to compensate its fiscal cost. Therefore, a government does not face conditions of increasing solvency and default risks. In contrast, if government deficit encourages debt-driven consumption and investment spending, then unsustainable growth may eventually cause a speculative government to shift to a Ponzi regime.

Evolutionary central banking: targeting speculative and Ponzi finance

Minsky's approach to central banking is grounded in his financial macroeconomic vision of the functioning of asset and liability creation-driven capitalist economies. It encompasses the dialectic between financial institutions and financial markets and the associate risks in a bank's asset and liability account balances from profit-seeking financial innovations, linkages and practices. The essentials just described motivated Minsky to elucidate the crucial role of the evolving legislated institutional structure that predisposes an economy's financial structure to fragility and instability. Minsky believed deeply in the authority of central banks to advance financial stability, macroeconomic coherence and economic progress.

For Minsky, central banking takes place in a complex environment. Micro-meso complexity involves liquidity and spending relations among banks, firms, households and governments. Note that these financial relations formulate the financial structure of effective demand. Organisations and financial markets evolve under permanent liquidity stresses, refinancing needs, solvency and default risks and position-making. Particular attention is paid to central banks' responsibility to intervene in the ordinary functioning of the financial system by creating liquidity processes to tolerate the validation of existing liability structures. Minsky (1986b, p. 359) upheld that

> central banking is a learning game in which the central bank is always trying to affect the performance of a changing system. Central banking can be successful only if central bankers know how the institutional structure behaves and correctly assess how changes affect the system. Central banks have to steer the evolution of the financial structure.

Above and beyond, Minsky (1977b) claimed that central banking is the art of regularly evaluating potential coordination failures of cash flows and the soundness of the balance sheet of financial organisations.

In this regard, one of Minsky's most useful insights is that the detection of speculative and Ponzi liability structures requires central banks to apply forward-looking evaluation processes of cash flows. These processes create valuable information about the impact of alternative monetary policy procedures on units' creditworthiness, credit risk and margins of safety. Most importantly, Minsky emphasised that in this evaluation processes, the key is the distinction between position-making operations that are collateral-based and income-based. It is presumed that, apart from the evolving macroeconomic conditions, a reliable assessment of a unit's liquidity position, default risk and refinancing capability depends on the dynamics of cash flows that result from its normal activities and/or from portfolio and balance-sheet transactions. In this regard, Minsky (1975a; 1982; 2013) prioritised the significance of the distinction between full employment and growth for central banks to evaluate the risk of position-making operations that are collateral-based and income-based. According to Minsky (1980a; 1980b), macroeconomic stability and order necessitate the continuous financing of capital development that engenders full employment with price stability under the supposition that these objectives can be accomplished and continued by robust financial market processes. In Minsky's system, as Tymoigne and Wray (2014) demarcated, economic growth might be unsustainable if it is driven by portfolio and balance-sheet transactions and especially by collateral-based speculative and Ponzi finance. In contrast, a full employment macroeconomic order that is achieved and sustained by income-based hedge finance is expected to be a robust and sustainable financial structure. As argued in the previous chapter, Minsky endorsed that income and cash flows that arise from production and distribution processes are low risk and sustainable. It is imperative to bring out that for Minsky, the fulfilment of payment commitments that relies on selling illiquid assets and on refinancing contains higher solvency and default risks than the fulfilment of payment commitments that is based on income flows from production and resource-creation processes.

In this context, Minsky recognised that the principal macro-objective of central banks should be full employment with price stability. This target necessitates central banks to initiate and put into practice monetary and financial instruments and procedures so as to create income flows and guarantee liquidity flows that promote developmentally friendly and stable financial structures. On these grounds, Minsky (1986b, p. 364) claimed that central banks need "to continuously 'lean against' the use of speculative and Ponzi finance". Hedge units contain income-based lending and their creditworthiness depends on income from normal operations. Collateral may still be required to set the margins of safety of a loan. However, its role is to decrease the credit risk of a bank instead of improving the capacity of units to service debt commitments. Alternatively, speculative, and especially Ponzi units, contain asset-based lending and their creditworthiness depends on variations in asset prices and the value of collateral. Furthermore, asset-based financing units must sell assets at a high price in order to have positive net worth to meet financial payments. Hedge units do not need to make new position-making operations. On the other hand, Ponzi finance relies on the capacity of units to refinance loans, and/or to liquidate asset positions in order to meet debt commitments.

Nonetheless, throughout his writings, Minsky depicted that speculative and especially Ponzi finance are the customary habits of financing of private investment-led growth processes in decentralised market economies. In particular, Minsky (1986b, p. 364) claimed that "capitalism without financial practices that lead to instability may be less innovative and expansionary; lessening the possibility of disaster might very well take part of the spark of creativity out of the capitalist system". This conception motivated him to accentuate that the substitution of an employment strategy for an investment strategy has to be the overriding goal of central banking to bring financial stability and order. In addition, he commented that central bank's endorsement of income-based hedge financing does not denote that collateral-based Ponzi and speculative financing will not come about. For this reason, Minsky believed genuinely that financial regulation is necessary to coerce commercial banks and other financial institutions to engage in underwriting methods that are conducive to hedge financing. If this type of underwriting becomes the predominant lending practice in banking, then the financial system would be more stable without large refinancing requirements for central banks to prevent a full-blown crisis. Therefore, for Minsky, the accomplishment of financial stability postulates the biasing of banks' financing towards employment and real-asset creation processes and the biasing of central banks' policy towards full employment.

Moreover, Tymoigne and Wray (2014) annotated that the ability of central banking to detect Ponzi liability structures presupposes that central banks evaluate the cash flows that indebted organisations use to repay debts rather than their ability to repay *per se*. The logic of this argument is that an organisation's capacity to fulfil financial commitments does not automatically involve low solvency risk, high margins of safety and financial robustness. For instance, a low solvency risk might be correlated with accessible refinancing sources because of higher value collateral-based assets. Therefore, low solvency risk is likely to dissimulate asset bubbles, unsustainable values of collateral-based assets and high default risk. On the other hand, high solvency risk might not be a warning of high default risk and financial fragility. The reason is that this high solvency risk might be the result of temporary fluctuations in income flows from production processes. Tymoigne and Wray (2014) remarked that the conditions that generate financial fragility risk are eventually connected with the degree that the available liquidity to organisations depends on future changes in incomes and in asset prices. The solvency risk of organisations varies because of their different reliance on refinancing and liquidation on non-monetary assets to meet debt commitments. Thus, the evolution of solvency risk and default risk is decidedly correlated with the quality of balance sheets, the open refinancing sources and the liquidation of non-monetary assets. However, the latter is not a normal and, certainly, cannot be a permanent source of cash inflows.

Units' refinancing risk capacitated Minsky to introduce the idea that, as Kregel (1992) marked out, central banks' solvency evaluation procedures should scrutinise an organisation's balance-sheet from assets to liabilities. In doing so, central banks should take pre-emptive measures to stabilise the prices of capital assets so as to ensure financial stability. In this respect, Tymoigne (2009) and Tymoigne and Wray (2014) noticed that despite the fact that capital and liquidity buffers on banks, deposit insurance mechanisms and lender-of-last-resort interventions are important elements of banking regulation and supervision, they might not be effective to deal with a unit's risk of position-making operations. Therefore, central bankers and regulators should take a more proactive and flexible approach to detect risky position-making operations that are correlated with financial innovations, changes in refinancing sources and channels and underwriting methods.

Another significant element of Minsky's core macro-theorisation of central banking is that the sustainability of cash flows from position-making that is collateral-based heavily hinges upon the existence of orderly secondary markets. Minsky frequently brought attention to the competence of economic units to sell assets in order to refinance their position-making. He claimed that this practice relies on whether purchased assets and liabilities are guaranteed sources of cash flows at guaranteed prices. To avoid solvency risk, organisations request assets that offer protection against temporarily disorganised asset markets. Minsky (1977b; 1979) anticipated that the central bank should be the institution that can guarantee the breadth, depth, and resiliency of a secondary market by choosing the instruments to finance position-takers in order to stabilise asset prices. In addition, he claimed that central banks should respond to disturbing fluctuations in the macroeconomic and financial environment and to counter-reactions by organisations. For Minsky, evolutionary central banking is even more crucial if new asset classes become important in units' portfolio preferences. Minsky (1977b) contemplated that secondary asset markets will be effective in stabilising the financial system only if they are adequately liquidated so as to orderly convert an asset into a reliable source of cash for an organisation's portfolio. The reliability of refinancing is ruled by the accessible liquidity sources and whether they are free from crisis of confidence in financial markets. Furthermore, the stability and order of new or inherited secondary markets depend on the set of protected assets that position-makers are able to acquire. But protected assets are the assets that are guaranteed by central bank's rediscounting procedures. In addition, if secondary markets cannot cope with the liquidity needs of organisations, then solvency risk would depend on their access to guaranteed refinancing especially when Ponzi and speculative finance is collateral-based. In this vein, Argitis (2017) argued that for Minsky, the central bank is the only institution that can guarantee this sort of asset protection and to assure reliable refinancing at the meso level. The reason is that a central bank is beyond doubt autonomous from financial markets regarding investors' revisions in portfolio risks and confidence that activate solvency risk and refinancing risk for organisations.

Minsky understood and endorsed that central banks' reliability and effectiveness in preserving orderly conditions in secondary markets hinge on its operational relations with position-makers. He believed that this interaction is very crucial for a central bank to be a reliable liquidity supplier to a wide variety of asset markets. This will advance the capability of central banking to guarantee a notable portion of the total reserve base of banks. For Minsky, this portion should be a key parameter of a central bank's policy discretion to target a wide range of assets eligible for discount. This type of meso discretion is vital for the solvency of the asset and liability structures at the micro level.

Stable monetary and financial systems

In Minsky's evolutionary approach to central banking, the functioning of the monetary and financial systems is fundamental since they are the institutions that create and allocate the liquidity needed by capital development. But, for Minsky, a market economy is inherently flawed and self-destabilising. Argitis (2013b) maintained that destabilisation would further escalate if wrong and inflexible rules, objectives and operational guidelines entrapped monetary and financial policies to self-regulated financial markets illusion and fine-tuning illusion.

As long as Minsky scrutinised the policy and institutional prerequisites for a successful variant of capitalism, he paid considerable attention to the distinction between an open market operation central banking and a discount window central banking. These two types of central banking are two monetary policy regimes. Minsky was concerned about which of these regimes is more conducive to financial stability and to 'real' resource-creation processes. Seen from another angle, Minsky scrutinised which of these monetary regimes could accomplish the overriding goal of full employment with price stability. Minsky (1986b) initially asserted that if a financial structure is being robust, then an open market operation central banking can be successful in stabilising the monetary and financial systems. His reasoning was that in a robust financial structure the speculative and Ponzi finance are an insignificant portion of the financing of positions in real assets. Besides, units are very likely to hold stocks of money and other liquid assets. In addition, Minsky claimed that a robust financial structure means that bank assets will be profoundly weighted by government debt and private debt held by hedge units. In these financing and liquidity conditions, it is apt for the central banks to target the reserve position of banks. Under such circumstances the available liquidity is indeed affected by open market transactions in which the central bank buys, sells, or accepts as collateral, Treasury debt. Besides, Minsky presumed that the cash which the units need to meet payment commitments does not increase significantly if interest rates increase. The reason is that in a robust financial structure private investment is primarily financed by investors' own funds. If bank financing is not the major determinant of investment spending, variations in reserves will not have a significant impact on the financial structure. Minsky (1977b) claimed that in such instances, central banking cannot control the liquidity supplied by decreasing bank reserves, as commercial banks and other financial institutions can substitute the private sector's debt for government debt in their portfolios. The consequence will be an increase in interest rates activated by the selling of government bonds in order for banks to create private debts. In this context, Minsky (1979) endorsed that in a robust financial structure, if central banks use open market operations to modify the reserve base and the financing supplied from banks they do not significantly affect the financing of private spending.

In addition, Minsky (1979) examined the case of a fragile financial structure. He asserted that in such a case, central banking must change the rules and the operations that were used when the financial structure was robust. The logic of his argument is that if public debt is not a significant position-making instrument, open market operations in Treasury securities are not a useful procedure and instrument to monitor the development of financial relations and linkages. Most importantly, they cannot guarantee the stability of the financial system. Bank reserves are correlated with the assets created by banks. But, if the central bank can intervene and co-finance the assets created, then reserves will change in relation to banks' asset structure and the private sector's demand for liquidity. Minsky (1979,

p. 81) held that "the supply of reserves must be linked to assets owned by banks and to assets that banks use in order to make position". In another passage Minsky (1986b, p. 361) noted that in a fragile financial structure "the central bank has a responsibility to operate to induce banks to hedge finance business. The authorities must look through the veil of the bank's balance sheet to the balance sheets of the organisations that the banks finance".

Throughout his writings, Minsky (1970; 1977b; 1979; 1986b) grasped financial stability to be more effectively accomplished if central banking shifts from monetary policy operations caught by the Treasury debt/open market operations base for the creation of the reserves towards a private debt/discount rate base. As was noted above, the Treasury debt/open market operation technique is appropriate for a robust financial structure where the assets acquired by banks are likely to include low risk and to be high market valued as collateral. The central bank needs only to conduct actions to influence the quantity of reserves without being concerned about banks' ability to finance the private sector. In contrast, when the financial structure is fragile, a central bank should apply its discretionary power to influence the reserves of banks stimulating them to promote hedge financing units and to discourage speculative and, especially, Ponzi financing units. This means that a central bank should encourage the use of short-term bank financing for the carrying of risk-free or low-risk assets so as to sustain the quality of asset and liability structures of banks. In this regard, central banking can influence the allocation of liquidity and take monetary policy decisions that institutionalise financing decisions that are associated with income creation and distribution processes. But this procedure postulates that a central bank does not solely use open market operations to control processes of selling and buying Treasury securities, but also operations that activate the discount window. Kregel (1992, p. 88) pinpointed that Minsky's support for the use of discount window

> is an attempt to introduce monetary policy at the beginning rather than at the end, of the process which determines capital asset prices, i.e. at the moment when banks and firms evaluate the future profitability of investment in drawing up lending agreements.

Furthermore, Minsky (1979, p. 86) designated that "the encouragement of this type of financing is a practical way of sustaining a degree of robustness to the financial structure", setting up "a financing relation between the central bank, the commercial banks and the various money market institutions". The discount window procedure safeguards the growth of the reserve base as a central bank accommodates the liquidity demands of banks and other financial institutions.

The importance of the discounting mechanism is that for any bank, liquidity will always be available at a price set by the central bank as long as banks acquired the specified type of assets. The type of assets that the central bank will have in its portfolio is a channel to control the supply of credit and the quality of position-making. Therefore, a discount window central banking is more effective to target the creation of hedge financing structures and the prevention of speculative and Ponzi financing. If banks increase the ratio of unprotected to protected assets in their portfolios, then they will face conditions of decreasing reserves. Besides, Minsky argued that once the central bank want to further boost the reserve base that was created by the discount mechanism, it can purchase Treasury bills from the open markets. Therefore, Minsky manifested that central banking must use flexible mechanisms to oversee and guide the evolution of economy's financial structure; and to avoid the rise of low-quality, unsustainable asset and liability structures. In this vein, Kregel (2013, p. 9) emphasised that Minsky endorsed that quantitative monetary policy must be replaced by qualitative monetary policy. Financial stability requires the formulation of a "new Qualitative monetary policy", which "reverse the concept of the lending the funds of depositors and recognise the importance of creating liabilities through the extensions of credit and the acquisition of assets" and examines "bank's balance sheets from assets to liabilities, rather than from liabilities to assets".

Furthermore, Minsky's conceptualisation of evolutionary central banking integrates the effectiveness of central banking with the effectiveness of fiscal policy. Central banking must be evolutionary so as to adapt to the evolving private sector's financial structure, to changes in government deficit and to the capacity of financial markets to absorb Treasury and private securities. Yet, as was argued above, in a capitalist economy with a big government, financial instability and debt-deflation might not occur as long as a big government runs deficits that can be financed in a way that it will not increase the interest rates and the liability pressures on portfolios. The financing of government deficit, through open market procedures in addition to the normal discount window channel, advances the sustainability of endogenous processes of cash flow creation and the quality of the private sector liability structures. Besides, by setting certain standards for eligibility to assets in order to be used as collateral at the discount window, central banking can endorse specific assets that desire to protect and investment plans that will finance. In this manner, discount window central banking could ameliorate the repercussions of a private investment-biased fiscal policy. Above and beyond, discount window central banking capacitated central banks to bypass banks and other financial institutions and directly finance private investment plans that promote employment and/or job creation public programs.

In this setting, Minsky conceived a tight monetary policy and high interest rates as disastrous for financial stability. High interest rates imply higher interest payments on rolled over debts. This then increases the likelihood of coordination failures of cash flows thus surging the indebted organisations' solvency and default risks. Under restrictive monetary conditions, organisations might be refinanced by emitting low-quality liabilities, selling assets and make risky changes in portfolios to offset the lower payment commitments anticipated in times of greater ease. Minsky asserted that tight money makes the financial system more fragile and augments the possibility for central banks to intervene as lender-of-last-resort in order to maintain asset prices and orderly market conditions. For Minsky (1979; 1986b), the lender-of-last-resort function of central banks should be complementary to the discount window central banking, and must come into play when certain classes of bank liability holders need protection against significant losses. Lender-of-last-resort interventions are effective when they target directly the purchase of assets of questionable value or the lending to risky position-making operations that are likely to default in order, as Fazzari and Minsky (1984) observed, to prevent a destabilising snowball of defaults and bankruptcies.

The lender-of-last-resort function takes as fact that the central bank has clearly approved the assets and markets that targets to protect. For Minsky, this operation is fundamental for achieving financial and macroeconomic stability, because central banks assure that refinancing does not collapse. However, this principle does not imply that the refinancing of particular business, households or branches of industry should not be interrupted. It is worth noting that Minsky admitted that lender-of-last-resort interventions probably raise moral hazard problems. In addition, he drew attention to the fact that they might stimulate the creation of risky financial innovations and assets. In this regard, Minsky (1960, p. 103) suggested that lender-of-last-resort functions should not be restricted to banks and financial institutions, but to include the entire economy. In particular, he argued that

> the bailing out action should be for the financial system, not for a particular unit. Individual lack of prudence should be punished by losses, but if the financial repercussions to such punishment threaten to be so wide that the probable result will be to induce a serious decline in investment and consumption, then the central bank must intervene.

Minsky (1979) claimed that central banking should examine the possibility of not to intervening and so let losses accumulate and organisations go bankrupt before beginning to refinance banks and other financial institutions. If a central bank intervenes to prevent financial instability by refinancing positions and protecting organisations, it may increase the possibility for them to continue to engage in risky position-making. As a result, in the future, units will be certain that the central bank will again intervene and protect their refinancing so they would feel sound to over-leverage. Therefore, if central banking quickly intervenes and validates possibly unsound financing practices that increase financial fragility and the possibility of a financial crisis, it is almost certain that it would generate the financial conditions for the next crisis. Nevertheless, Minsky (1986b) believed that the longer a central bank delays its intervention the larger the effects would be on financial stability, economic activity and employment. Accordingly, lender-of-last-resort functions are important but only in a monetary and financial environment in which central bank's major concern is to continuously dampen those activities that lead to speculative and Ponzi finance and to sustain hedge finance. As a final point, it is worth mentioning that the effectiveness of lender-of-last-resort practices to sustain asset values depends on the size of the government and on the government debt and deficit. In an economy with a big government the failure of the central bank to maintain asset values and to stabilise the financial system might not have the negative effects that would have been prevalent in the case of a small government and deficit.

Subsequently, central banks must target the stability of monetary and financial systems. They should take pre-emptive measures in order to avoid the deterioration in the quality of leverage and the solvency of the liability structures. This is more probable to occur in the institutional structure of a discount window central banking. In addition, central banks and financial regulators must select a measure of leverage that, as Tymoigne and Wray (2014) argued, accounts for not only the size of the leverage, but also its quality that is defined by the expected reliance on refinancing and liquidation of assets in order to service debt commitments. When solvency-risk and default-risk upsurge, central banking has limited power to prevent financial instability, because of the low quality of leverage. An essential precondition for central banks to detect, manage and control speculative and Ponzi position-making transactions is the institutionalisation of a qualitative monetary policy and a proactive, flexible and evolving system of regulation.[12] Such a system can, early on, detect risky financial innovations that boost risky refinancing sources and stimulate underwriting methods that undervalue solvency risk and safety margins. The early detection of financial fragility necessitates interventions that control the risky asset creation processes and prevent collapses of market values especially under circumstances that the traded assets are not protected by the central bank's discount window.

Conclusions

Minsky's financial macroeconomics postulates that if the financial system is left to its own dynamics, then, most probably, it will intensify rather than mitigate the instability inevitably created by endogenous forces in market economies. Following Keynes's political economy, Minsky claimed that economic policy is an inescapable determinant of macroeconomic evolution, because it shapes the institutional framework that conditions the structure and functioning of the financial and business sectors. Since this institutional structure continuously changes, economic policy must evolve and adjust in order to sustain and improve economic security, prosperity and stability. In Minsky's macro-vision, the preconception of laissez-faire is absent, while fine-tuning is impossible. Market economies are at best 'conditionally coherent'.

Stabilisation policy should contain institutions and interventions that substitute certainty for uncertainty. However, the foregoing discussion has shown that for Minsky, institutions and interventionist policies are incapable of enduringly stabilising the financial and macroeconomic systems and eradicating the defects of the market economies. They can simply set ceilings and floors to control their 'natural' instability. The institution of Big Government functions as a significant automatic stabiliser of the expenditure system for the private sector which boosts output and prices, and, to some extent, can counterbalance the fall in profits and cash flows that emanate from lower levels of private spending. Minsky contemplated that fiscal authorities instead of using the general government spending targeting private investment and, possibly jobless, inflationary growth, to bring into effect 'employer of last resort' programs to achieve tight, full employment without inflation, and to endorse better wage and income equality. Furthermore, he invigorated the setting of governmental deposit insurance regulatory structures. Finally, Minsky favoured evolutionary central banking as an institutional adaptation process in which discount window procedures, lender-of-last-resort interventions and co-financing of hedge units could be used to formulate a qualitative monetary policy. The latter should target the eradication of speculative and Ponzi leverage and the activation of employment and resource-creation processes. He grasped these monetary and financial instruments and procedures to be indispensable for central banks to prevent the collapse of asset values and to promote full employment with price stability.

Notes

1 For an insightful discussion of Keynes's political economy see Dillard (1946; 1948) and Darity (1995).

2 It must be stressed that Minsky (1996, p. 364) acknowledged that his political thinking was inspired by Henry Simon's political economy and his idea that the major goal of economic policy must not be narrowly economic. Minsky pinpointed that according to Simon "the aim of policy is to assure that the economic prerequisites for sustain the civil and civilised standards of an open liberal economy exist. If uncertainty is amplified, extremes of income distribution and, and social inequality attenuate the economic underpinnings of democracy, then the market behavior that creates these conditions should be constrained. It is necessary to give up a bit of market efficiency, or a bit of aggregate income, in order to contain democracy-threatening uncertainty, then so be it".

3 In Chapter 17 of the *General Theory*, Keynes (1936) scrutinised how the own-rate of interest on money 'rules the roost' and illustrated its 'predominating practical importance' in considering the change of fundamental macroeconomic variables (see e.g. Dillard, 1948; 1980; 1986; 1987; Davidson, 1978; Rotheim, 1981; Kregel, 1982; 1983; 1985; Minsky, 1985–1986).

4 This insight depicts Gesell's influence on Keynes's social and political philosophy (see e.g. Dillard, 1942; 1946; Darity, 1995; Argitis, 2008–2009). In *The Natural Economic Order* Gesell (1934) demonstrated his vision of socio-economic reforms. Gesell considered money and the monetary system as instruments of power that cause market dysfunctions. Gesell perceived the monetary system as a structural defect of capitalism and as a structural barrier to the continuous full employment of resources.

5 It is worthy to note that Minsky disputed the theoretical foundations of neoclassical-Keynesianism and its policy prescriptions that emphasise the 'fine-tuning' of aggregate demand and the promotion of private investment (see e.g. Ferri and Minsky, 1989). Argitis (2013b) stated that, according to Minsky, the 'fine-tuning illusion' emanates from the mistaken notion of conventional macroeconomics that the incoherence of financial capitalism is attributed to institutional rigidities, and not to fundamental uncertainty and to the endogenous nature of financial instability.

6 For Minsky (1996, p. 367) "a full employment economy is supportive of democracy".

7 The following passage discloses the political economy of his anti-poverty strategy. Minsky (2013, pp. 1–2) maintained that "the war against poverty must not depend solely, or even, primarily, upon changing people, but it must be directed toward changing the system. However, the changes required are not those that the traditional radicals envisage. Rather, they involve a commitment to the maintenance of tight full employment and the adjustment of institutions, so that the gains from full employment are not offset by undue inflation and the perpetuation of obsolete practices".

8 In Minsky's conceptual system, conventional ideas and policies which claim that the credibility of governments should be evaluated by their commitment to inflation-targeting and that the unemployment is the inevitable cost of low inflation are out of place. They are appraised as destabilising and socially destructive (see e.g. Argitis, 2013b).

9 Minsky's ELR proposal has been discussed at length and further developed and refined by numerous theoretical and empirical studies. For a more detailed clarification of Minsky's insights and of the conceptual, operational and practical elements of ELR programs see e.g. Antonopoulos et al. (2014), Bell and Wray (2004), Papadimitriou (1998; 2008), Tcherneva (2012; 2018), Wray (1997; 1998; 2000; 2007b; 2016).

10 In my point of view, this insight has crucial implications for industrial relations, because the minimum wage is constantly disputed by neoclassicism and neo-liberalism.

11 In this regard, Wray (2000) claimed that an ELR policy might not completely stabilise the overall price level, as it is not a substitute for an incomes policy.

12 For Minsky's view of banks, banking and financial regulation see e.g. Minsky et al. (1993), Kregel (2014) and Wray (2016).

5 Cultural financial foundations for evolutionary macroeconomics

Introduction

Conventional macroeconomic theory, in all its variants, is incapable of sufficiently addressing the real facts of economic experience, in particular the explosive dynamics and the debt-deflation tendencies of an accumulating capitalist economy with complex, evolving and unstable financial markets. What is needed is the disengagement of the macroeconomic theory and policy from the habits of thought and the routinised fundamentals of neoclassical scholarly wisdom; and the incorporation of the essential characteristics of the cultural and structural changes in the financialised capitalist economies in which we live. As was underlined in the introduction of this book, the inversion of the habitual way of theorising requires the recontextualisation of macroeconomics.

The thesis of this book is that a recontextualisation of macroeconomics presupposes the institutionalisation of new habits of thought and analytical routines that coincide with the realities of the concrete economic world. To grasp the complexities of the maturing finance capitalism a restatement of basic assumptions is needed. My argument is that Veblen's and Minsky's 'anti-equilibrium', anti-laissez-faire and pro-institutional theories provide foundations that can advance the level of pragmatism in macroeconomics. The aim of this chapter is to display a core of insights and causal factors led down by Veblen and Minsky that depict three foundational principles for an evolutionary macroeconomic theory and policy: the holistic nature of macroeconomics, where attention is paid to the evolving financial institutions; the unsustainable leverage and liability structures induced by pecuniary habits and values, speculative and parasitic credit creation and solvency illusions; and the cultural foundations of the principle of the parasitic and insufficient demand, which engenders industrial inefficiency, waste, inequality and unemployment. These foundational principles mix together Veblen's post-Darwinian cultural, holistic macroeconomics with Minsky's Schumpeterian financial macroeconomics.[1] This mixture establishes a cultural, financial and processual approach to the interconnection among an economy's financial structure, aggregate demand and macroeconomic performance and brings about certain institutional reforms and interventions to promote community's welfare.[2]

Evolutionary macroeconomics as a part of cultural, holistic economics

Following Veblen, evolutionary macroeconomics is the study of the macro-system as an ongoing process of adaptation to a larger and evolving social and economic order. The latter, as Gruchy (1987) has underlined, is a cultural pattern with a past, present and future. An economy is a structurally interrelated whole whose many sub-systems are functionally interdependent. Each sub-system must be examined within the context of the cultural whole in which its functions. According to this principle, the macro-system cannot be adequately explained until its connections to the rest of the socio-economic system will have been thoroughly analysed. In this conceptual framework, macroeconomics is part of an evolving historico-cultural structure, whose functioning forms the prevailing habits of mind, routines and customs.

The financial macroeconomic visions of Veblen and Minsky advance the pragmatic bias of this holistic outlook to macroeconomics. Their enduring contribution is that they bring to the surface the evolving financial structure and the need to be incorporated into an evolutionary theorisation of macroeconomics. The evolving financial structure reflects the continuous and cumulative changes in the industrial, business and financial environments under the pressure of the growing financial institutions. One of Veblen's fundamental presumptions is that the evolution of pecuniary institutions causes a cultural anti-industrial bias that destabilises the macro-system. The institutional structure brings about behaviours and decisions, which, ultimately, govern the complexity of income flows, cash flows and the flows of the goods and services required by the financial and macroeconomic systems to be in order and by the community to meet its welfare standard. In other words, the subject matter of cultural, evolutionary macroeconomics is the examination of how the fittest habits of thought in banking and finance and the outcome of the conflict between the instinct of workmanship and the pecuniary and emulative instincts rule a capitalist economy's cyclical trends, growth and welfare potentials. Veblen's essential contribution is that the macro-system is driven by the inauguration, selection and institutionalisation of habits of mind and routines that are embedded in a larger socio-economic and cultural system. Minsky's contribution is that financial entrepreneurship, innovation and competition typify these habits and routines that manifest themselves in a variety of financial and macroeconomic behaviours and performances, i.e. different leverage structures, debt/income ratios, growth rates, unemployment rates, etc.

There are some basic preconceptions and presumptions which underlie the pragmatic bias of this holistic, evolutionary theorisation of macroeconomics. A first point to emphasise is that, in contrast to habitual macroeconomics, the subject matter of macroeconomic analysis is not the study of the efficient allocation of resources, but the qualitative depiction of macroeconomic change in light of the predominant habits and routines in finance and banking; and their impact on industrial efficiency, waste and social provisioning.[3] The evolution of financial institutions matters because it determines the productive or the parasitic allocation of liquidity and the use of credit. The principle of solvency rules the market valuation processes of units' balance sheets that influence banks' decisions over the allocation of liquidity. The institutionalisation of certain financial habits of thought and norms follows the building of organisations' leverage and liability structures. Veblen and Minsky have underlined the importance of financial exigencies that triumph when the growth of financial markets accelerates the accumulation of debt and the building of liability structures. Men's habits of thought change under the pressure of financial exigencies. The expansion of debt and the development of risky financial innovations and predatory money-managing processes habitualise pecuniary values and practices in business and banking and behaviours motivated by predatory and emulation instincts. Behavioural adjustments of individuals, social groups and organisations, at the micro-meso levels, define the process of selection of habits of thought, conventions and customs of conduct, which are passed on to the other sub-systems of an economy, through adaptive processes regarding financial contracts and arrangements.

Financial innovations and competition form a selection mechanism of habits and routines that order the endogenous processes of credit creation and layering. This then, in combination with pecuniary liquidity allocation procedures, make the sub-systems of an economy and the interdependence of the cash flows of organisations more structurally and functionally interrelated. These norms eventually rule the conditions that bring about consistency and coordination, or inconsistency and coordination failure among the various sub-systems, particularly among industry, business, finance and economic policy. A ground to understand this complexity is Minsky's coordination failure of cash flows. Evolutionary macroeconomics postulates that cultural consistency is a prerequisite for Minsky's coordination of income and cash flows that ensures macroeconomic coherence and stability. In contrast, cultural inconsistency disharmonises coordination of income and cash flows and destabilises the financial and macroeconomic systems. Therefore, evolutionary macroeconomics diagnoses that cultural inconsistency erodes the coherence of an evolving macro-system influencing the balance between the productive and parasitic growth of the layering of liability structures and of aggregate spending. The evolution of pecuniary habits of mind induces changes in the proportion of income transactions to the balance-sheet transactions and portfolio transactions that fashion conditions of insolvency and of a systemic financial disorder. Note, emphasis is paid on the financial interpretation of the cultural incoherence of a market economy as an originator of solvency, liquidity and default risks. Evolutionary macroeconomics accentuates the cultural basis of Minsky's 'survival constraint' illustrating that the aggregate demand is predisposed to insolvency and an unsustainable financial structure.

Another point to stress is that in a structurally interrelated credit economy, there is a fundamental disharmony of interests underlying the operations of its various sub-systems as a going concern. In Veblen's vision, the statement of a pre-existing harmony of economic interests is unquestionably incorrect. Besides, the premise of conflict or harmony of interests becomes dependent upon the prevailing institutions and business principles. It is worth noting that in evolutionary financial macroeconomics, the notion of cultural harmony differs from the habitual concept of equilibrium. As mentioned, harmony is brought about by a number of inter-related factors in industry, business and finance and embraces habits of thought, inertia, vested interests, power and collective action. Concern should be drawn to the evolving complexity of units, corporations, banks, trade unions, governmental agencies and monetary authorities. Their structure of interlinks and interactions changes in accordance with cultural conditions, the distribution of power and the evolving market processes.

It is important to underline that a core element of evolutionary financial macroeconomics is Veblen's dualism between income and pecuniary values and between workmanship and predation. However, as it will be discussed below, this dualism frames the micro-meso-macro environments, which eventually influence the coordination of income and cash flows and the evolving solvency regimes of organisations. It must be highlighted that the ultimate direction of macroeconomic change is uncertain. Financial macroeconomic stability or instability will eventually be governed by the degree that the income-creation and distribution processes will be subordinated to business and pecuniary values and principles.

Another important aspect of the holistic and processual theorisation of macro-economics is Veblen's premise that cultural evolution dominates human mind prior to decisions taken in various spheres in industry, business and banking. But, these decisions fashion innovations, structures and markets, which, in turn, insti-tutionalise certain habits of thought and routines. Therefore, institutions disregard the behavioural assumption used by habitual macroeconomics concerning the universalising acultural homo economicus. This then invalidates the hypothesis about the intertemporal predominance of market forces in the comprehension of macroeconomic change. In this regard, one of Veblen's most useful contributions is the illumination of the way that the financial aspects of cultural evolution para-sitise the spending of investors and consumers. Cultural patterns of behaviour demoralise unrealistic assumptions about rational agents who optimise utility and profit functions under perfect or bounded information and knowledge.

From this cultural standpoint, evolutionary macroeconomics underlines the need to grasp the cause and effect of the interconnectedness of finance, indus-try, economic policy and politics. Above and beyond, the evolving institutional patterns of financial macroeconomic relations, which are not of a standardised character all over the capitalist economies, formulate the basis for a Veblenian cultural recontextualisation of macroeconomics. Since there is not cultural homogeneity, macro-behaviour breaks down into a variety of cultural-financial spheres which vary among countries. Macroeconomic analysis should explain change in every particular cultural structure. Most importantly, evolutionary macroeconomics should concentrate on the institutions that cause and retard change in economic growth and community's welfare. Attention must be focused on how different conditions of culture and power can alter the struc-ture and functioning of the macro-system and its capacity to promote social provisioning. This institutional analysis could be further extended to incorpo-rate even more complex international cultural structures.

Pecuniary and economic values, coordination failure of cash flows and financial fragility

Having a strong pragmatic bias, the holistic, evolutionary outlook to financial macroeconomics seeks to accomplish the aim of a more realistic theorising of the recurrent episodes of over-leverage, deleverage, financial crashes and debt–deflation. Veblen and Minsky presume that these episodes are due to, among other factors, the structure and functioning of the financial system. As stated in previous chapters, a credit-driven capitalist economy is established by complex borrowing and lending relations, which depend upon anticipations of the organisations' evolving solvency and margins of safety. MFIH (Minsky's 'financial instability hypothesis') uncovers the financial preconditions and scrutinises solvency as a valuation process of changes in the price systems in the goods, labour and financial markets. VFIH (Veblen's 'financial instability hypothesis') goes much deeper and exposes the cultural foundations of solvency. The central presupposition is that the prevailing pecuniary habits of mind relegate industrial efficiency and institute the price systems of goods, labour and assets as the coordinator of pecuniary efficiency. But, if industrial efficiency is replaced by pecuniary efficiency as the predominant principle in the processes of making income and cash flaws, the sustainability of solvency diminishes. For Veblen, the institution of the price systems contemplates the cultural interdependence among solvency, business capital and industrial capital. On this ground, solvency relies on the co-evolution among the industrial, business and financial systems, which initiates variations in the price systems. These variations are the quantitative reflection of the institutional changes that rule the processes of creating pecuniary and economic values. The growth of pecuniary institutions boosts the processes of creating pecuniary values. In this cultural framework, solvency is a fundamental precondition for the smooth functioning of financial markets and the price systems. But, solvency has a pecuniary and elusive character and is used to evaluate the efficiency of business capital, not the efficiency of industrial capital.

As analysed, economic values are real or tangible values, which are created by industrial processes in the form of commodities or services that meet personal and social needs. In contrast, pecuniary values are exchange values derived by market forces, which reflect the dynamics of business traffic. Persistent discrepancies between the streams of economic and pecuniary values disclose the liquidity misallocation and the distribution inefficiency caused by the predominant financial institutions. It must be stressed that the emphasis on income inequality is because of its direct correlation with industrial inefficiency. Veblen hypothesised an inverse relationship between the distributional repercussions of the pecuniary use of leverage and industrial efficiency. The higher is pecuniary debt, the higher income inequality, parasitic spending and insufficient demand become. In other words, income inequality evidences pecuniary efficiency, while the latter augments Minsky's coordination failure of cash flaws. In this respect, Veblen underlined the importance of tangible investment for industrial efficiency and the creation of economic values. On the other hand, Minsky stressed that the refinancing of a unit becomes dependent upon the margins of safety that are embodied in the solvency of its income-flows dynamics to validate the inherited debt structure.

As a result, a key insight of evolutionary macroeconomics regards the relationship among tangible investment, the creation of economic values, the sustainability of income flows and the solvency of balance sheets of the various organisations (business firms, households, banks, government). It is hypothesised that the impact of the aforementioned micro-financial dynamics on Minsky's well-known hedge, speculative and Ponzi solvency regimes becomes dependent upon the meso-macro cultural consistency or inconsistency. Each of these regimes is determined by the dynamics of the economic value and pecuniary value creation processes in the form of cash flows from income production and distribution processes and from balance sheet and portfolio transactions. Therefore, the classification of a financial structure as robust or fragile depends on the predominant habits of mind and the routines that structure pecuniary norms of financing and parasitic spending.

The critical postulation is that competition and imitation among organisations is very likely to upsurge the leverage and liability structures beyond the limit required by industrial efficiency. The accumulated pecuniary debt boosts business capital. Consequently, an imbalance between economic and pecuniary values comes about. However, the growth of pecuniary leverage deteriorates an economy's actual and potential growth rates and capacity to engender sustainable income and liquidity flows. Moreover, a higher pecuniary leverage increases the market value of collateral that can be, speculatively, used for new position-making and refinancing. The mixture of pecuniary recapitalisation and leverage elucidates the cultural and pecuniary nature of financial fragility and instability. As financial institutions and banking grow and liquidity is not allocated and used to finance productive activities, industrial inefficiency, insolvency and financial fragility become possible. The institutions of manipulation and fraud emerge as principles of pecuniary success in manipulating the solvency risk. They are used to give wrong information and to create illusions about the quality of balance sheets and about biased solvency rankings.

Veblen's q ratio constitutes a significant contribution to evolutionary macroeconomics. It captures the evolving balance between tangible and intangible assets and exposes the dynamics of biased solvency evaluations and of pecuniary efficiency. A higher q ratio results from a pecuniary restructuring of capital due to the speculative accumulation of intangible assets. The unpreventable accumulation of pecuniary capital advances the market value of collateral and escalates refinancing. At the same time, it discourages the growth of tangible assets and the creation of sustainable cash flows activated by industrial processes of income creation. In addition, the growth of pecuniary over-leverage augments the imbalance between economic and pecuniary values, making more likely a liability structure to become an unbearable real debt burden. If an increased volume of business capital is collateralised by securities that are not backed by actual tangible assets, solvency might collapse and coordination failures of cash flows would come about. Veblen and Minsky anticipate that a collapse of solvency activates deleverage and increases the likelihood of a liquidity crash. This result could be avoided only if there are institutions that ensure stability and order at the meso-macro levels.

By remarking this principle, evolutionary macroeconomics conceptualises pecuniary and speculative over-leverage as an indication of a parasitic use of credit that would, in due course, initiate solvency, liquidity and market risks. Over-leverage and deleverage are envisaged as cultural-financial processes that institutionalise cycles of parasitic adaptation of capital. At the macro level, this adaptation evolves through processes of euphoria, booms, speculative crashes, financial fragility and instability and debt-deflation. The coherence between the macroeconomic and financial systems is therefore susceptible to the predominant pecuniary habits and routines. The emphasis of evolutionary macroeconomic scrutiny should not be on macroeconomic order and harmonious productive, technological and financial relationships, but rather on macroeconomic disorder and the repercussions of the evolving financial institutions and the predominant predatory instincts and habits.

Effective demand, waste and full employment

Evolutionary macroeconomics explores the cultural nature of community's welfare. The latter is presumed and is best served by a higher production of economic values in the form of serviceable goods and by the efficient working of the productive system at its full employment capacity. But industrial efficiency is eroded by the cultural inconsistency among finance, business and industry that induces an unsustainable effective demand, which causes persistent divergences between actual and potential growth rates. This growth gap contemplates the cultural basis of the interdependence between aggregate supply and effective demand in market economies. In line with the visions of Veblen and Minsky, evolutionary macroeconomics postulates the significance of the distinction between economic growth and full employment. The reasoning is that a full employment income-creation process is an indispensable precondition for organisations to generate sustainable income and cash flows to maintain their solvency and refinancing.

In contrast, an under-full employment economic growth indicates a state of insufficient demand and income-creation processes that render organisations incapable of engendering sustainable income and cash flows so as to preserve their solvency and refinancing. Therefore, persistent divergences between actual and potential growth rates signify possible grounds of financial fragility and disorder. On the other hand, financial order and stability become dependent upon liquidity creation and refinancing processes that keep the effective demand close to full employment. In this context, an under-full employment growth is associated with unsustainable dynamics of layering and spending, as well as with potential coordination failures of cash flows. Units' insolvency risk activates endogenous micro-meso liquidity distress and defaults that are likely to trigger insufficient demand, involuntary unemployment and debt-deflation at the macro level.

On these grounds, evolutionary macroeconomics integrates the evolving financial structure with the determinants of the aggregate demand. Attention is paid to the effect that pecuniary debt exerts on the sustainability of the liability structures created by units to finance their spending. A liability structure creates streams of payment commitments on debts which are, or not, validated by income flows, such as wage and other household incomes, gross profits after taxes for business and taxes for governments. A major hypothesis is that an increasing pecuniary debt brings about waste and insufficient demand. Therefore, for evolutionary financial macroeconomics, the evolving pecuniary habits and routines parasitise the financing and spending decisions of bankers, investors and consumers dropping private aggregate spending below the level required to promote full employment. Note, parasitic financial manoeuvres and wasteful private spending elucidate the cultural and pecuniary character of effective demand. In addition, they bring to the fore the inability of private, and especially unregulated, markets and of the price systems to achieve industrial and distribution efficiency.

Macroeconomic under-performance proves that resources, liquidity and income are not allocated in a balanced and efficient manner so as to minimise waste and maintain high levels of aggregate demand and serviceable output. Parasitic spending, which is directly associated with conspicuous and emulative consumption and intangible investment denote pecuniary efficiency, waste and insufficient demand. In particular, conspicuous and emulative consumption satisfy the predatory instincts of the leisure class. It is parasitic spending on the purchasing of non-serviceable, luxury and high-status goods and services, which do not satisfy human needs and promote social provisioning. In this regard, evolutionary financial macroeconomics hypothesises a significant correlation among income inequality, parasitic consumption spending, insufficient demand and an under-full employment growth. These cultural dynamics of the effective demand are further uncovered by examining a debt-driven investment. Minsky illustrated the destabilising financial dynamics of investment that emanate from a higher debt leveraging for corporations and banks. In a Kaleckian-Minskyan framework, an increase in leverage boosts investment, effective demand and profits. If leverage is driven by over-optimism and solvency illusions, then the inherited debt structure might cause liabilities to increase at a faster rate than investment increases income inflows. Furthermore, in Keynes's monetary system, a higher debt/income ratio and high interest payments are expected to redistribute capital income towards rentiers and the elite of finance. This distribution effect reduces entrepreneurial income, liquidity and investment, and, unless compensated by other profit inducing spending, the aggregate capital income. MFIH illustrates the solvency effect of the declining profits and cash inflows.

Veblen's distinction between investment in tangible and intangible assets uncovers the cultural origins of the evolving financial structure of investment. In addition, it adds significant dynamics into the endogenous processes that cause insufficient demand and insolvency in market economies. Tangible investment expenditures induce all the positive, Kaleckian-Minskyan type effects on productivity, employment, effective demand and profits. Nevertheless, the structure of investment is fundamental for the creation and distribution of profits and the sustainability of cash inflows realised by organisations. When there is a continuous inadequacy of tangible investment, the aggregate private demand cannot absorb the output produced by the industrial sector. As a result, profit and cash flows realisation problems come about. This principle indeed implies that the share of intangible to total investment spending is directly correlated with the coordination failure of cash flows that invalidates the confidence of risk-adverse businessmen and bankers. A fall in aggregate profits displays the likelihood of organisations having been engaged in parasitic spending and leverage structures. The higher solvency risk of liability structures increases the risk of debt payment commitments not to be validated and the possibility of deleveraging beginning so as to circumvent default risk. In this regard, evolutionary macroeconomics should pay significant attention to the structure of investment due to its role as a major determinant of the streams of income flows that validate the liability structure of organisations.

Furthermore, the dynamics of the co-evolution between the financial structure and effective demand change if an increase in consumption spending by households is debt-financed. In such a case, the relation between consumption spending and effective demand becomes financially more complex and uncertain, whereas it is liable to changes in income distribution. The cash flows that validate household's debt come from their disposable income, mainly from wages. If the wage income falls short of the anticipated wage income, then this reduction, according to Minsky, is likely to transform a hedge financing household into a speculative or Ponzi financing one. Thus, any change in income distribution at the expense of wages negatively affects, apart from consumption and saving, household's competence to meet debt commitments. An important aspect of Minsky's analysis is that the solvency regime of a household depends on the portion of speculative and Ponzi financing in economy's financial structure. If a speculative increase in the asset creation process happens, a household probably increases its debt/income ratio because of higher market value of collateral. However, household's wage income might not be adequate to meet the outstanding payment commitments. In such a case, the posture of a household's financing regime depends on the sustainability of asset prices. It will also be susceptible to changes in monetary policy and the financial environment. The financial structure of effective demand becomes even more complex after the incorporation of government debt. Government units are, usually, speculative financing units. If the total future expected cash inflows – mainly from taxes net of current expenses – exceeds the total future cash payment commitments on the outstanding debt, there are not solvency risk and roll over problems. Nevertheless, high interest rates and high primary deficits can transform speculative, especially non-sovereign, government units into Ponzi units. This development might reduce government expenditures and hence aggregate spending.

For evolutionary macroeconomics, the validation of the total debt for an economy, or for sub-sectors, is an evolving process that relies on whether various components of national income are sustainable. This principle secures that the maturing debt commitments will be fulfilled either out of profits, wages, taxes, etc., or out of refinancing. The latter depends on the anticipated solvency risk and the margins of safety of units. Solvency problems induce default risk and reduce the quality, and hence the sustainability, of the financial structure of effective demand. In a demand-driven market economy the quality of balance sheets relies on various structural, policy and institutional variables that promote and stabilise income-creation processes. In this framework, there is a permanent problem of insufficient demand in market economies due to endogenous fragility and instability of the financial structure. Pecuniary debt and risky and profit-seeking financial interrelations engender income redistribution changes that parasitise a part of aggregate demand. Insufficient demand is an obstacle to income and employment creation activities that secure solvency. In this approach, the detection of balance-sheet problems by investors causes severe repercussions for the solvency and credit rating of banks, firms, households and governments. A revision of the solvency risk affects the validation of an economy's debt and spending structure.

The political ideology and the macro-sociology of an evolutionary macroeconomic safety net

The macro-visions of Veblen and Minsky provide the institutional foundations for an anti-laissez-faire social philosophy of evolutionary macroeconomics. The thrust of this philosophy is that major ills of market economies, such as speculative over-leverage, deleverage, unemployment, insecurity, inequality and debt-deflation are credited, to a significant degree, to the evolving financial institutions that establish the supremacy of pecuniary efficiency. Another equally important implication is that capitalism cannot by itself create an institutional and financial structure that could enduringly eliminate instability and promote full employment economic growth, equality and social cohesion. Therefore, it is necessary to build a framework of institutional reforms and interventions biased towards the protection of industrial efficiency and full employment. In this regard, the building of a macroeconomic safety net emerges as an indispensable precondition of a market economy to achieve a mutual coexistence between the productive and financial structures and to accomplish the needs of social provisioning. This safety net should institutionalise market and governmental processes that will induce: liquidity allocation efficiency and distribution efficiency by promoting a higher level of non-conspicuous consumption and investment in tangible productive capital; sustainable asset and liability structures; solvency and financial stability; and a higher volume of targeted effective demand that will permanently push employment close to full employment.

A first point to underline is that this safety net should continuously adapt to the growing financial, economic and social institutions. This principle implies that a program of fiscal, monetary and financial reforms can only be effective only as a part of a general system of institutional reforms that copes with the macro-sociology of institutional evolution. For evolutionary macroeconomics, this macro-sociology governs the supply-side constraints and demand-side shortages that rule the creation and sustainability of income and cash flows that determine the order and stability of an accumulating capitalist economy. In other words, the fundamental goal of an effective macroeconomic safety net is the demotion of the growth of pecuniary institutions that function as a structural barrier to full employment. Evolutionary macroeconomics should therefore be biased against any institutional structure that encourages the creation of pecuniary values and the promotion of pecuniary efficiency.

This approach to the macroeconomic safety net is based on Minsky's insight about the 'conditional coherence' of market economies. As a result, for evolutionary macroeconomics, a great deal of emphasis should be placed on the detection of the institutions and the intrinsic speculative and Ponzi financial processes that destabilise the market economies, and on the manifestation of the institutions and policies that humanise their stabilisation. It is hypothesised that the greater the proportion of private intangible investment and conspicuous consumption in aggregate spending, the greater the weight of speculative and Ponzi finance in financial structure. This hypothesis, which blends VFIH and MFIH, implies that a private aggregate spending boom is destabilising because it is very likely to be susceptible to solvency illusions and failed margins of safety. Thus, an effective macroeconomic safety net should entail a pro-employment and productive spending bias. This aim can be accomplished if the legislated institutional structure tolerates the implementation of a program of institutional reforms and interventions that target the lessening of parasitic spending and the promotion of full employment.

At this point, it should be recognised that the political economy of evolutionary macroeconomics opposes the vested interests and pecuniary practices of the elite of business and finance. Furthermore, the overruling macro-sociological goal of an effective safety net should be the institutionalisation of the instinct of workmanship. Workmanship obliges norms of thought and routines that promote technological change and productivity, industrial efficiency and the creation of economic values. This appears to be a fundamental prerequisite for market economies to disapprove pecuniary efficiency and values. In addition, the institutionalisation of the instinct of workmanship is a means of adapting the mentality of policy-makers to learning processes and habits of mind that legitimise employment, community's well-being and distribution efficiency. Above and beyond, the institutionalisation of the instinct of workmanship is imperative for building a mutual co-evolution between financial and industrial systems. In this regard, evolutionary macroeconomics demonstrates the holistic interdependence of the supply-side and the demand-side of an economy.

Following Veblen, the supply-side reflects the state of the industrial arts, which establishes the important role of technology, knowledge and of popular education in an economy's productive capacity. Moreover, in a workmanship-driven accumulating economy, the price systems of labour, goods and assets will be used to rate industrial efficiency in terms of employment and social provisioning. An increase in wages will be favourably evaluated in terms of a higher effective demand and industrial efficiency. The lower the income inequality is, the lower the share of income that goes to vested interests and to parasitic spending is. Therefore, evolutionary macroeconomics postulates that there is a positive relation between distribution efficiency and industrial efficiency. Income equality evidences industrial efficiency, financial stability and higher effective demand and growth rates.

Consequently, the growth of employment and productive activity is an ongoing cultural process of habits, ideas, attitudes and beliefs that presuppose the institutionalisation of the instinct of workmanship. This principle should govern the macroeconomic safety net so as to target the promotion of non-pecuniary spending and the activation of processes that advance employment and sustain income and cash flaws. In such a cultural setting, regulatory structures that devitalise the 'invisible hand' are significant for policy-making to control speculative private debt-ratios, fraud, manipulation and unsustainable liability structures. They are also imperative for improving the allocation efficiency of liquidity. In addition, governments and central banks should fashion procedures and interventions to control parasitic behaviour and expenditures and stabilise and encourage employment and income flows creation processes.

An evolutionary targeting approach to macroeconomic policy

Evolutionary macroeconomics entails an evolutionary targeting approach to fiscal policy and central banking. The major idea is that economic policy should target the control of parasitic spending and of unsustainable asset and liability structures; and the creation of institutions that promote full employment and sustainable income and cash flows. Such policy interventions prevent solvency and liquidity crises and foster prudent balance sheets. The completion of these objectives requires an evolutionary adaptation of stabilisation policy to the endogenous multi-unit productive and pecuniary structures of an evolving debt-driven market economy. Hence, evolutionary targeting is at odds with the static, rule-and-expectations-creation approach to policy-making proposed by the habitual macroeconomic theory.

Minsky's cash flow method of detecting speculative, Ponzi and hedge financing is at the epicentre of this evolutionary targeting approach. Evolutionary adaptation should focus on institutional reforms and interventions directed at varying areas of failure at the micro-meso-macro levels that creates the 'survival constraint' of organisations and the enduring coordination failure of cash flaws. Evolutionary targeting is the art of detecting and selecting out of a set of various spending categories, debt/ratios, solvency and liability structures and income-creation processes the ones to be targeted and appropriately managed. The process of detection and selection is very important especially in transition periods towards speculative and Ponzi led leverage and liability structures, where banking crutches, financial fragility and asset-bubbles are likely to come about. It is worth noting that for both Veblen and Minsky, interventionist policies are impotent to permanently eradicate the defects of the market economies. They can only set ceilings and floors to control their 'natural' instability.

In the realm of fiscal policy, the evolutionary targeting approach underlines the necessity of a counter-cyclical government budget to cope with effective demand gaps that emanate from insufficient private spending. Fiscal policy is visualised as the art of deliberately manipulating the government spending and taxation so as to offset the fall in income flaws – in the form of profits, wages and public revenues – which stem from lower levels of private spending. A downside variability of these income flaws would probably induce coordination failures of cash flows and solvency, liquidity and default risks for units at the micro-meso levels. In addition, fiscal policy should initiate practices that allocate resources towards the activation of employment and resource-creation practises.

It is significant to underline that the habitual counter-cyclical government spending increases the aggregate demand and, in a Kaleckian manner, the corporate profits, but its effect on the allocation of profits among organisations and between financial and non-financial units is uncertain and uneven. The profit and job creation in some sectors might benefit or be damaged more than other sectors as a result of a general increase or decrease in government spending. Besides, it is not certain that an increase in profits and cash flows will stabilise the balance sheets of speculative and Ponzi units. It is more sensible to argue that the hedge units are more likely to get the bigger share in the distribution of the created profits. Thus, although that the institution of Big Government indeed ensures that aggregate corporate profits and solvency do not fall, as Minsky has pointed out, it cannot guarantee that within the corporate and banking sectors there are not units that fail to validate their debt and margins of safety. Moreover, as was pointed out, habitual counter-cyclical fiscal policy might fail to promote, via market processes, adequate job creation and mostly to secure full employment, whereas it is likely to induce significant inequalities in income distribution between high- and low-wage paid workers. In a Veblenian context, the job and output creation impact of a pro-private-investment-driven growth fiscal policy is uncertain, because the higher aggregate demand may validate a higher rate of accumulating intangible capital.

In this vein, the overriding goals of an evolutionary targeting approach to fiscal policy in debt-driven capitalist economies are the advance of industrial efficiency and the promotion of full employment.[4] This guiding principle in the formulation of a counter-cyclical fiscal policy presupposes the restructuring of government spending and the targeted progression of public spending categories that induce significant positive effects on tangible investment, on job creation for particular unemployed groups and to households who are unable to meet their debt commitments. The merit of a directed government spending is that it might have an immediate positive impact on specific industries that accumulate tangible capital and products that satisfy human needs. Positive feedback effects on industrial and distribution efficiency boost the sustainability of income and cash flows and hence the validation of an economy's debt structure. However, the final allocation of profits and of income flows among units is accomplished by the price systems and decentralised market mechanisms. In this regard, the pre-determined allocation of income and cash flows in favour of potentially insolvent firms and households is rather uncertain.

Nevertheless, a pro-employment restructuring of fiscal spending, in the form of Minsky's employer of last resort strategy, appears to be a more realistic one in influencing income-creation processes. Note, for evolutionary macro-economics, the closing of the employment gap evidences financial macroeconomic stability and coherence. In addition, it is an indication of reducing pecuniary efficiency and increasing distribution, allocation and industrial efficiency. The justification is that by employing the unemployed, fiscal policy stabilises and creates income and cash flaws for low-income social groups that increase the aggregate demand, mostly, for the industries that produce goods and services which satisfy human needs.

In this evolutionary approach to fiscal policy, Minsky's three stabilising effects of government deficit, namely the income and employment effect, the budget effect and the portfolio effect are fundamental. Sustainable income and cash flows improve units' debt-carrying capacity and margins of safety and the quality of private portfolios, which continuously adjust to the evolving balance between protected and unprotected assets. Evolutionary macroeconomics hypothesises that an increase in non-pecuniary government deficit increases the weight of protected government assets in private portfolios and hence prevents downward pressures on financial and capital asset prices, especially if they are backed by tangible assets. In this context, non-pecuniary and directed government spending, deficit and debt activate ceilings and floors in the product, labour and financial markets that constrain the endogenous instability of market economies. They appear to be fundamental preconditions for a financially robust growth. In this regard, an evolutionary fiscal policy puts emphasis on tangible investment and employment-creation processes that simultaneously increase aggregate demand and supply at a higher level of a non-inflationary social provisioning. In addition, the sustainability of income flows supported by directed resource-creation processes advance government's solvency and refinancing. For evolutionary macroeconomics, a solvency and liquidity crisis is controllable if all economic sectors' debt contracts are fulfilled and if income and cash flows are sustained by non-parasitic counter-cyclical government deficits.

Nevertheless, the delegitimisation of pecuniary efficiency cannot be achieved only as a result of a reorientation of the structure of government expenditures. An evolutionary targeting approach to central banking is also fundamental for enlarging the macroeconomic safety net in a way that it would better improve industrial efficiency and the liquidity allocation efficiency. The foregoing discussion has shown that over-leverage and deleverage are major features of speculative financial processes that cause coordination failures of cash flows and insolvent and unsustainable balance sheets. The principal objective of evolutionary central banking should be the prevention of the emergence of speculative and, especially, Ponzi financial structures. An evolutionary targeting central banking is the art of detecting risky financial innovations and pecuniary and predatory financial habits and routines. The pre-selection of qualitative leverage, liability and fragility indexes for the household, business, financial and government sectors are essential benchmarks for evolutionary targeting central banking so as to control the risky asset and liability creation processes. The aim is to prevent insolvency and default risks that would induce collapses of asset values. A qualitative monetary policy and a proactive, flexible and evolving system of regulation can control speculative refinancing sources and imprudent underwriting methods, which undervalue solvency risk and safety margins.

Evolutionary central banking focuses attention on central banks' responsibility to intervene in the ordinary functioning of the financial system by creating liquidity processes at the micro-meso levels to tolerate refinancing and the validation of liability structures. The creation of liquidity channels should consider the dynamics of cash flows that emanate from organisations' normal activities and/or from portfolio and balance-sheet transactions. Hedge units contain income-based lending and their creditworthiness depends on income flows that arise, possibly, from non-parasitic operations. Speculative and especially Ponzi units use asset-based lending and their solvency relies on the stability of financial markets. Fluctuations in asset prices and the value of collateral determine the solvency and creditworthiness of speculative and Ponzi units, which might have been engaged in pecuniary and non-sustainable operations. For this reason, evolutionary central banking should activate regulatory structures that would make commercial banks and other financial institutions engage in underwriting methods that promote tangible investments and non-parasitic consumption spending. If this type of non-pecuniary underwriting becomes the principal lending practice in banking, then the weight of hedge units in the financial structure might upsurge. In addition, a non-pecuniary underwriting advances the liquidity allocation efficiency. The latter is a precondition for financial stability and order, since it minimises the refinancing requirements for central banks to prevent a full-blown liquidity crisis. Therefore, the achievement of financial macroeconomic coherence becomes dependent upon the biasing of central banking towards full employment and tangible-asset creation processes that generate sustainable income and cash flows.

Another significant element of evolutionary central banking is the acknowledgment that the solvency of balance sheets depends upon the presence of orderly secondary markets. Refinancing and recapitalisation rely on whether purchased assets and liabilities, as Minsky pinpointed, are guaranteed sources of cash flows at guaranteed prices. Minsky often observed that organisations, in order to avoid solvency risk, demand assets that offer protection against temporarily disorganised asset markets. The trustworthiness of accessible liquidity sources depends on whether secondary markets are free from crisis of confidence that is on the volume of protected assets that speculative and Ponzi position-makers are able to obtain. But, as mentioned, protected assets are the assets that are guaranteed by central bank's rediscounting procedures. Therefore, for evolutionary central banking, the portion of protected assets to total assets should be a targeted, pre-selected financial ratio. It must be a key parameter of a central bank's qualitative monetary policy discretion, aiming to target the financing of job creation public programs and income-creation tangible assets eligible for discount. Under such circumstances, discounting could be a monetary tool for central banking to advance the liquidity allocation efficiency and to promote tangible investment and employment.

This evolutionary meso-discretion is a pre-requirement for the solvency of the asset and liability structures at the micro level, especially if the financial structure is fragile. Therefore, evolutionary central banking implies that central banks must apply their discretionary power to influence the reserves of banks motivating them to endorse hedge financing units and to dampen speculative and, especially, Ponzi financing units. In this regard, central banking can make a significant contribution to the augmentation of the macroeconomic safety net towards the institutionalisation of the instinct of workmanship and the financing of employment and income-creation processes. The use of discount window is a concrete way of supporting the robustness of the financial structure. This occurs because liquidity will be provided to any bank as long as it acquires protected assets and finances non-parasitic spending. Therefore, a discount window central banking is more effective to anticipate the rise of speculative and Ponzi financing. Therefore, central banks should use flexible procedures to supervise and control the evolution of an economy's financial structure, and to prevent the escalation of low quality, unsustainable balance sheets. The discount window procedures together with lender-of-last-resort interventions can approve a range of assets and of secondary markets that central banks would target to protect. Closing, evolutionary central banking should be an institutional adaptation process in which discount window procedures, lender-of-last-resort interventions and financing of non-parasitic spending formulate a qualitative monetary policy that should target the suppression of speculative and Ponzi leverage and the activation of employment and resource-creation processes.

Conclusions

Following Veblen and Minsky, evolutionary macroeconomics points out that once the process of macroeconomic evolution is viewed from the cultural, financial sphere of influence, macroeconomic theory and economic policy turn out to be cultural, evolutionary and holistic. Modern macroeconomics must therefore draw particular attention to the evolving institutional environment and the cultural relationships that govern macroeconomic and financial processes, practices, decisions and behaviour. The structure and functioning of the industrial, business and financial systems engender certain habits of thinking and routines, which cumulatively and selectively come to form the institutional setting that rules the structure of technological, financial and distribution relations.

Evolutionary financial macroeconomics is groping towards a vision where macroeconomic change is seen in terms of the impact that the established habits of thought, embodied in the evolving financial institutions, have on industrial and pecuniary efficiency, waste, effective demand, employment and growth. It is mostly argued that the evolution of pecuniary finance has separated the business and banking sectors from industry. The growth of business capital dishonours industrial capital and weakens businessmen's determination to serve a full employment economic growth and community's welfare. It is postulated that if markets, and especially financial markets, were left to their own endogenous processes, they would amplify the fragility and the incoherence created by cultural, financial dynamics. In this regard, evolutionary financial macroeconomics aims to draw out the institutional essentials of financial fragility and instability and the endogenous nature of macroeconomic incoherence of market economies, where all capital asset positions depend upon the quality of leverage and liability structures. Unsustainable income and cash flows lead organisations to fail to validate past spending decisions and future payment commitments. Capitalism inherently tends towards insufficient demand, waste, involuntary unemployment, income inequality and poverty.

Macroeconomic stabilisation policy is a fundamental feature of macroeconomic evolution, because it affects the institutional framework that conditions the structure and functioning of the industrial, financial and business sectors. Since this institutional structure continuously and cumulatively changes, macroeconomic policy must evolve and adjust in order to sustain stability, order and prosperity. In this setting, evolutionary macroeconomics provides useful insights that could substantiate a program of reforms and interventions that would establish a cultural consistency among the various sub-systems of a market economy along the following fundamental principles: in a debt-driven capitalist economy private markets and the price systems fail to allocate resources, liquidity and income in a balanced, efficient and an equitable manner so as to sustain high levels of aggregate demand and economic activity. In contrast, productive and full employment creation processes deliver equity, industrial efficiency, stability and coherence. The establishment of institutions that habitualise the instinct of workmanship can increase industrial efficiency and activate endogenous financial and macroeconomic stabilising processes. Financial institutions, tangible investment financing and social provisioning cannot be left to unregulated and self-adjusting markets. The elimination of waste and the promotion of a full employment effective demand require an efficient allocation of liquidity and of income distribution. The reduction of the parasitic share of income is necessary to invalidate wasteful spending. The increase in the income share of the efficiency experts and workers is necessary to validate productive spending and the debt structure.

A crucial aspect of evolutionary macroeconomics is that there is a high interdependence between the supply- and the demand-side of an economy. The supply-side reflects the state of the industrial arts and the importance of technological progress. In this context, a successful program of reforms should concentrate on the building of institutions that endorse a virtuous, mutual symbiosis between productive and financial structures from which people derive their livelihood. The growth of non-pecuniary financial institutions can advance the cultural authority of economic values and the principle of workmanship on the macro-system. In this setting, institutional intervention and fiscal and monetary policies should activate productive processes and sustainable income and cash flows so as to push the macro-system close to full employment. Policy institutions, and especially governments and central banks can control parasitic behaviour and expenditures and limit the destabilising tendencies of capitalist economies. However, the most crucial objective is to establish a workmanship-led regime of a full employment aggregate demand, financial stability, robust economic growth and social provisioning.

Concluding, the recontextualisation of macroeconomics should include the culturalisation of macroeconomics. The latter can be done if the macroeconomic system is conceptualised as an ongoing cultural process which is under the influence, among other factors, of financial institutions embedded in a larger social, economic and cultural process. This macroeconomic approach places markets, values, power, prices, and all macro-variables in a historico-cultural setting rather than in the acultural setting of the rational individual behaviour in the market system of habitual macroeconomics.

Notes

1   There are significant theoretical and policy cross-linkages and common denominators in Veblen's and Minsky's financial macro-visions, see e.g. Kelso and Duman (1992) and Argitis (2013a). Nonetheless, it must be underlined that "there are differences in the scope, details and emphasis between Veblen's system and Minsky's system. In most respects, Veblen goes further and deeper than Minsky in drawing out the institutional essentials of the financial fragility and instability within the business enterprise system. But, in the analysis of the financial sector, Minsky not only adds much sophistication to the work of Veblen, but he is truly innovative with regard to the underlying reasons for which we observe financial fragility in modern capitalism" (Argitis, 2013a, p. 39).
2   Post-Keynesian and original Institutionalist authors have made significant contributions to the understanding of macroeconomics as a processual and financial framework of interpretation of real-world economies; see e.g. Peterson (1977; 1987), Adams (1980), Wilber and Jameson (1983), Keller (1983), Dillard (1980; 1986; 1987), Gruchy (1987), Hodgson (1989), Niggle (2006), Whalen (1996; 2008; 2011).
3   The concept of social provisioning implies that any socio-economic and cultural order has to induce market and non-market activities and production, distribution and consumption processes so as to provide the flow of goods and services that is required for carrying out community's needs and well-being (see e.g. Gruchy, 1987; Dugger, 1996; Todorova, 2013).
4   The evolutionary targeting approach to fiscal policy presented here is a Veblenian contextualisation of Tcherneva's (2012) bottom-up approach to fiscal policy.

Epilogue

Severe systemic financial fragility and macroeconomic instability have become apparent as the finance-driven transformation of modern markets economies takes place. The last global financial crisis was a result of a significant speculative bubble that has caused a crisis of confidence, destabilising contemporary capitalism. The creation of highly leveraged and unregulated financial markets has brought about huge financial risks, defaults, stagnation tendencies and social insecurity. Inequality, jobless recovery, tangible disinvestment, parasitic leverage and speculative and trading banking formulate gloomy prospects and display stresses and strains that raise questions about the sustainability and the democratisation of finance capitalism. The political economy of reforming contemporary capitalism principally implies the creation of a new institutional and financial structure that would erase the barriers towards economic and social progress.

This book argues that a concrete examination of the aforementioned phenomena presupposes the development of an evolutionary financial macroeconomic theory and policy. Such a theory sets forth the pragmatic basis to grasp the peculiar and evolving nature of finance capitalism; to understand the major aspects and the origins of financial instability and crisis and of the macroeconomic underperformance of market economies; and to develop an agenda of reforms and interventions to stabilise and democratise modern economies and societies. Evolutionary financial macroeconomics elucidates how the behaviour of asset-and-liability-driven capitalist economies is critically affected by the way in which pecuniary institutions govern the evolving structure of capital and the solvency and coordination of income and cash flows that influence aggregate demand and the validation of the inherited debt. Essentially, any evolutionary macro-system reflects the co-evolution among the productive and financial structures and economic policy-making. It was precisely this holistic approach that Veblen was preoccupied with in his cultural macroeconomic vision. Evolutionary financial macroeconomics identifies the cause and effect of the macro-inefficiency in the interplay between pecuniary institutions and tangible investment that rules the degree of interdependence between production, distribution, financing and spending. An interdependency that is determined not only by market processes, but also by pecuniary evaluations of the price systems that principally reflect the evolution of culture.

Cultural evolution brings to the fore the role of the habitual frame of mind in household, business, banking and government decision-making processes. The escalation of pecuniary institutions into the common sense of finance-driven capitalist economies downgrades productive norms that are no longer self-evident, and, furthermore, routinises speculation, over-leveraging, bubbles, frauds and waste. The outcome is the activation of endogenous processes of financial macroeconomic incoherence. The cultural origins of the allocation of resources and liquidity as well as of the distribution of income disclose the dynamics of insolvent leverage and liability structures. Financial fragility and instability, debt-deflation, business cycles and depression are conceptualised as path-dependent developments. This vision enables evolutionary financial macroeconomics to anticipate the repercussions of financialisation and to point up the need for reforming the institutional and financial structure of modern capitalist economies. A solvency crisis, a deleveraging shock of a deflationary nature and a boost in parasitic spending destabilise the financial and macroeconomic systems in the absence of income and cash flows stabilisers. The latter raised the task of the overriding objectives of an evolutionary targeting macroeconomic policy that should be the protection and progress of social provisioning. By taking into account this principle, evolutionary financial macroeconomics accentuates the macro-sociology of the adaptation of economic policy to the prevailing instincts and institutions. Indeed, it is important to stress that for evolutionary macroeconomics, institutional reforms and interventionist policies are incapable of enduringly stabilising the financial and macroeconomic systems and removing the flaws of the accumulating and financially sophisticated capitalist economies characterised by private property. Stability is not an inherent property of the capitalist system, but the conditional effect of institutional adaptations and policy interventions. A fundamental feature of capitalist reality is its evolving complexity and multiplicity.

The development of a post-Darwinian, cultural and finance-led processual approach to macroeconomics comprises a contribution to the advance of a broader cultural, holistic method of understanding economic and social change. Nonetheless, the further development of a cultural, holistic approach to macroeconomics requires inputs from other traditions, in particular from the evolutionary, the Post-Keynesian and the original institutionalist ones. The emphasis this book paid on financial institutions and structures does not imply in any way that evolutionary macroeconomics relegates to a second order of concern the importance of technological progress and the production and organisational processes, which bears directly upon the structure and functioning of an economy and its macroeconomic system. In this respect, the contributions of the neo-Schumpeterian evolutionary economics to the analysis of the micro-meso-macro environments are imperative. They can help to exemplify the evolution of habits and routines advancing the cultural, holistic approach to macroeconomics.

Furthermore, for evolutionary macroeconomics, incomes policy emerges as indispensable for financial stability and sustainable growth. An incomes policy must seek to create income and cash flows without triggering inflationary problems aiming to ensure the solvency of households and a change in income distribution towards more equity. Incomes policy interventions must be made before solvency and fragility issues come into sight. In a debt-driven economy, the main objective of such a policy should be to inject purchasing power and cash flows into the industrial and financial structures So, evolutionary macroeconomics should incorporate innovational empirical investigations of the financial macroeconomic implications of the labour market institutions and especially of the collective bargaining system and the minimum living wage. The reinforcement of these institutions would improve not only the strength of organised labour in income distribution, but also the income and cash flows necessary for financial macroeconomic stability.

The pragmatic bias of the evolutionary holistic outlook to macroeconomics can be further augmented by theoretical and empirical research in the direction of the instinctual and habitual foundations of consumer's, investors' and government's complex spending behaviour. In this regard, the evolutionary macroeconomic analysis is necessary to endorse contributions from other disciplines such as cultural anthropology, economic sociology and evolutionary psychology. The aforementioned fields of study call into play a few more directions leading to a new research approach that could invigorate the pragmatism of macroeconomics so as to push it towards more non-dogmatic, real-world dimensions.

References

Adams, J. (ed.) (1980). *Institutional Economics: Contributions to the Development of Holistic Economics*, Boston: Martinus Nijhoff Publishing.

Anderson, K. (1933). "The unity of Veblen's theoretical system", *The Quarterly Journal of Economics*, 47(4), pp. 598–626.

Antonopoulos, R., Adam, S., Kim, K., Masterson, T. and Papadimitriou, D.B. (2014). "Responding to the unemployment challenge: A job guarantee proposal for Greece", Research project report, Annandale-on-Hudson, NY: The Levy Economics Institute of Bard College.

Argitis, G. (2008–2009). "Inflation targeting and Keynes's political economy", *Journal of Post Keynesian Economics*, 31(2), pp. 249–270.

Argitis, G. (2013a). "Veblenian and Minskian financial markets", *European Journal of Economics and Economic Policies: Intervention*, 10(1), pp. 28–43.

Argitis, G. (2013b). "The illusions of the 'New Consensus' in Macroeconomics: a Minskian analysis", *Journal of Post Keynesian Economics*, 35(3), pp. 483–505.

Argitis, G. (2016). "Thorstein Veblen's financial macroeconomics", *Journal of Economic Issues*, 50(3), pp. 834–850.

Argitis, G. (2017). "Evolutionary finance and central banking", *Cambridge Journal of Economics*, 41(3), pp. 961–976.

Argitis, G. and Nikolaidi, M. (2014). "The financial fragility and the crisis of the Greek government sector: A Minskian analysis", *International Review of Applied Economics*, 28(3), pp. 272–291.

Atkinson, G. (2007). "Pecuniary institutions: Their role and effects", in J.T. Knoedler, R.E. Prasch and D.P. Champlin (eds.), *Thorstein Veblen and the Revival of Free Market Capitalism*, Cheltenham: Edward Elgar, pp. 69–86.

Ayres, C.E. (1958). "Veblen's theory of instincts reconsidered", in D. Dowd (ed.), *Thorstein Veblen: A Critical Reappraisal*, New York: Cornell University Press, pp. 25–37.

Bell, S. (2003). "Common currency lessons from Europe: Have member states forsaken their economic steering wheels?", in L-P. Rochon and M. Seccareccia (eds.), *Dollarization: Lessons from Europe and the Americas*, London: Routledge, pp. 70–91.

Bell, S. and Wray, L.R. (2004). "The war on poverty after 40 years: A Minskyan Assessment", Public Policy Brief No. 78, Annandale-on-Hudson, NY: The Levy Economics Institute of Bard College.

Bellofiore, R. and Ferri, P. (eds.) (2001). *Financial Keynesianism and Market Instability: The Economic Legacy of Hyman Minsky*, 2 vols, Cheltenham, UK: Edwar Elgar.

Bolbol, A.A. and Lovewell, M.A. (2001). "Three views on stock markets and corporation behaviour: Tobin, Veblen and Marx", *Journal of Post Keynesian Economics*, 23(3), pp. 527–543.

Brown, D. (ed.) (1998). *Thorstein Veblen in the Twenty-First Century*, Cheltenham, UK: Edward Elgar.

Burlamaqui, L. (2000). "Schumpeterian competition, financial innovation and financial fragility: An exercise in blending evolutionary economics with Minsky's macro-finance", paper given at the 8th Schumpeter Conference, Change, Development and Transformation, Manchester, UK, 28 June–July 1st.

Burlamaqui, L. and Kregel, J. (2005). "Innovation, competition and financial vulnerability in economic development", *Brazilian Journal of Political Economy*, 25(2), pp. 5–22.

Cornehls, J. (2004). "Veblen's theory of finance capitalism and contemporary corporate America", *Journal of Economic Issues*, 38(1), pp. 29–58.

Darity, W. (1995). "Keynes's political philosophy: The Gesell connection", *Eastern Economic Journal*, 21(1), pp. 27–41.

Daugert, S.M. (1950). *The Philosophy of Thorstein Veblen*, New York: Columbia University, King's Crown Press.

Davidson, P. (1978). *Money and the Real World*, London: Macmillan.

Dente, L. (1977). *Veblen's Theory of Social Change*, New York: Arno Press.

Dillard, D. (1942). "Silvio Gesell's monetary theory of social reform", *American Economic Review*, 32(2), pp. 348–352.

Dillard, D. (1946). "The pragmatic basis of Keynes's political economy", *The Journal of Economic History*, VI(2), pp. 121–152.

Dillard, D. (1948). *The Economics of John Maynard Keynes: The Theory of a Monetary Economy*, New York: Prentice-Hall.

Dillard, D. (1980). "A monetary theory of production: Keynes and the institutionalists", *Journal of Economic Issues*, 14(2), pp. 255–273.

Dillard, D. (1986). "The institutional principle of the principle of economics", *Journal of Economic Issues*, 20(2), pp. 355–363.

Dillard, D. (1987). "Money as an institution of capitalism", *Journal of Economic Issues*, 21(4), pp. 1623–1647.

Dimand, R.W. (2004). "Echoes of Veblen's theory of business enterprise in the later development of macroeconomics: Fischer's debt-deflation theory of great depressions and the financial instability theories of Minsky and Tobin", *International Review of Sociology*, 14(3), pp. 461–470.

Dirlam, J. (1958). "The place of corporation finance in Veblen's economics", in D. Dowd (ed.), *Thorstein Veblen: A Critical Reappraisal*, New York: Cornell University Press, pp. 199–219.

Dopfer, K. (ed.) (2001). *Evolutionary Economics: Program and Scope*, Dordrecht: Kluer Academic Publications.

Dopfer, K. (2005). "Evolutionary economics: A theoretical framework", in K. Dopfer (ed.), *The Evolutionary Foundations of Economics*, Cambridge, UK: Cambridge University Press, pp. 3–55.

Dopfer, K. (2012). "The origins of meso economics: Schumpeter's legacy and beyond", *Journal of Evolutionary Economics*, 22(1), pp. 133–160.

Dopfer, K. and Potts, J. (2008). *The General Theory of Economic Evolution*, Abingdon: Routledge.

Dopfer, K., Foster, J. and Potts, J. (2004). "Micro-meso-macro", *Journal of Evolutionary Economics*, 14(3), pp. 263–279.

Dorfman, J. (1934). *Thorstein Veblen and His America*, New York: Viking Press.

Dowd, D. (ed.) (1958). *Thorstein Veblen: A Critical Reappraisal*, New York: Cornell University Press.

Dugger, W.M. (1996). "Redefining Economics: From Market Allocation to Social Provisioning", in C. Wallen (ed.), *Political Economy for the 21st Century*, Armonk, New York: M.E. Sharpe.

Dymski, G.A. and Pollin, R. (1992). "Hyman Minsky as a hedgehog: The power of the Wall Street paradigm", in S. Fazzari and D.B. Papadimitriou (eds.), *Financial Conditions and Macroeconomic Performance: Essays in Honor of Hyman P. Minsky*, New York: M.E. Sharpe, pp. 27–61.

Dymski, G.A. and Pollin, R. (eds.) (1994). *New Perspectives in Monetary Macroeconomics: Explorations in the Tradition of Hyman P. Minsky*, Ann Arbor: University of Michigan Press.

Edgell, S. (1975). "Thorstein Veblen's theory of evolutionary change", *American Journal of Economics and Sociology*, 34(3), pp. 267–280.

Fagerberg, J. (2003). "Schumpeter and the revival of evolutionary economics: An appraisal of the literature", *Journal of Evolutionary Economics*, 13(2), pp. 125–159.

Fazzari, S. and Minsky, H. (1984). "Domestic monetary policy: If not monetarism, what?", *Journal of Economic Issues*, 18(1), pp. 101–116.

Fazzari, S. and Papadimitriou, D.B. (eds.) (1992). *Financial Conditions and Macroeconomic Performance: Essays in Honor of Hyman P. Minsky*, New York: M.E. Sharpe.

Ferrari-Filho, F., Terra, F. and Conceição, O. (2010). "The financial fragility hypothesis applied to the public sector: An analysis for Brazil's economy from 2000 to 2008", *Journal of Post Keynesian Economics*, 33(1), pp. 151–168.

Ferri, P. and Minsky, H. (1989). "The breakdown of the IS-LM synthesis: Implications for post-Keynesian economic theory", *Review of Political Economy*, 1(2), pp. 123–143.

Ferri, P. and Minsky, H. (1991). "Market processes and thwarting systems", Working Paper No. 64, Annandale-on-Hudson, NY: The Levy Economics Institute of Bard College.

Foster, J. (2000). "Competitive selection, self-organization and Joseph A. Schumpeter", *Journal of Evolutionary Economics*, 10(3), pp. 311–328.

Foster, J. (2011). "Evolutionary macroeconomics: A research agenda", *Journal of Evolutionary Economics*, 21(1), pp. 5–28.

Ganley, W. (2004). "The theory of business enterprise and Veblen's neglected theory of corporation finance", *Journal of Economic Issues*, 38(2), pp. 397–403.

Gesell, S. (1934). *The Natural Economic Order: Money Part*, San Antonio: Free Economy Publishing Company.

Gruchy, A. (1958). "Veblen's theory of economic growth", in D. Dowd (ed.), *Thorstein Veblen: A Critical Reappraisal*, New York: Cornell University Press, pp. 151–176.

Gruchy, A. (1967). *Modern Economic Thought: The American Contribution*, New York: Augustus M. Kelley Publishers.

Gruchy, A. (1987). *The Reconstruction of Economics: An Analysis of the Fundamentals of Institutional Economics*, New York: Greenwood Press.

Hake, E. (2007). "Capital and the modern corporation", in J.T. Knoedler, R.E. Prasch and D.P. Champlin (eds.), *Thorstein Veblen and the Revival of Free Market Capitalism*, Cheltenham: Edward Elgar, pp. 31–68.

Hall, J., Dominguer-Lacasa, I. and Gunther, J. (2012). "Veblen's predator and the great crisis", *Journal of Economic Issues*, 46(2), pp. 411–418.

Hamilton, D. (1974). *Evolutionary Economics. A Study of Change in Economic Thought*, Albuquerque: University of New Mexico Press.

Henry, J. (2012). "The Veblenian predator and financial crises: Money, Fraud, and a world of Illusion", *Journal of Economic Issues*, 46(4), pp. 989–1006.

Hobson, J.A. (1936). *Veblen*, London: Chapman and Hall.

Hodgson, G.M. (1988). "On the evolution of Thorstein Veblen's evolutionary economics", *Cambridge Journal of Economics*, 22(4), pp. 415–431.

Hodgson, G.M. (1989). "Post-Keynesianism and institutionalism: The missing link", in J. Pheby (ed.), *New Directions in Post-Keynesian Economics*, Aldershot: Edward Elgar, pp. 94–123.

Hodgson, G.M. (1992). "Thorstein Veblen and post-Darwinian economics", *Cambridge Journal of Economics*, 16(3), pp. 285–301.

Hodgson, G.M. (2004a). "Veblen and Darwinism", *International Review of Sociology*, 14(3), pp. 343–361.

Hodgson, G.M. (2004b). *The Evolution of Institutional Economics: Agency, Structure, and Darwinism in American Institutionalism*, London and New York: Routledge.

Keller, R. (1983). "Keynesian and institutional economics: Compatibility and complementarity", *Journal of Economics Issues*, 17(4), pp. 1087–1095.

Kelso, P.R. and Duman, B.L. (1992). "A Veblenian view of Minsky's financial crisis theory", *International Journal of Social Economics*, 19 (10 November 2012), pp. 222–234.

Kelton, S. and Wray, L.R. (2009). "Can Euroland Survive?", Public Policy Brief No. 106, Annandale-on-Hudson, NY: Levy Economics Institute of Bard College.

Keynes, J.M. (1923). *A Tract on Monetary Reform* (CW: IV), London: Macmillan.

Keynes, J.M. (1934). *Poverty in Plenty: Is the Economic System Self-Adjusting?* (CW: XIII), London: Macmillan.

Keynes, J.M. (1936). *The General Theory of Employment, Interest and Money*, Cambridge: Macmillan and Cambridge University Press.

Knoedler, J.T., Prasch, R.E. and Champlin, D.P (eds.) (2007). *Thorstein Veblen and the Revival of Free Market Capitalism*, Cheltenham: Edward Elgar.

Kregel, J.A. (1982). "Money, expectations and relative prices in Keynes' monetary equilibrium", *Economie Appliquée*, 35(3), pp. 449–465.

Kregel, J.A. (1983). "Effective demand: Origins and development of the notion", in J.A. Kregel (ed.), *Distribution, Effective Demand and International Economic Relations*, London: Macmillan.

Kregel, J.A. (1985). "Hamlet without the prince: Cambridge macroeconomics without money", *American Economic Review*, 75(2), pp. 133–139.

Kregel, J.A. (1992). "Minsky's 'two price' theory of financial instability and monetary policy: Discounting versus open market intervention", in S. Fazzari and D.B. Papadimitriou (eds.), *Financial Conditions and Macroeconomic Performance: Essays in Honour of Hyman P. Minsky*, New York: M.E. Sharpe, pp. 85–103.

Kregel, J.A (1997). "Margins of safety and weight of the argument in generating financial fragility", *Journal of Economic Issues*, 31(2), pp. 543–548.

Kregel, J.A. (2007). "The natural instability of financial markets", Working Paper No. 523, Annandale-on-Hudson, NY: The Levy Economics Institute of Bard College.

Kregel, J.A. (2008). "Minsky's cushions of safety: Systemic risk and the crisis in the U.S. subprime mortgage market", Public Policy Brief No. 93, Annandale-on-Hudson, NY: The Levy Economics Institute of Bard College.

Kregel, J.A. (2013). "We need a 'New Q': Replace quantitative with qualitative monetary policy", paper given at the 22nd Annual Hyman P. Minsky Conference on the State of the US and World Economies, Building a Financial Structure for a Stable and Equitable Economy, Annandale-on-Hudson, NY: The Levy Economics Institute of Bard College.

Kregel, J.A. (2014). "Minsky and dynamic macroprudential regulation", Public Policy Brief No. 131, Annandale-on-Hudson, NY: The Levy Economics Institute of Bard College.

Lawson, C. and Lawson, L. (1990). "Financial system restructuring: Lessons from Veblen, Keynes and Kalecki", *Journal of Economic Issues*, 24(1), pp. 115–131.

Lawson, T. (2015). "Process, order and stability in Veblen", *Cambridge Journal of Economics*, 39(4), pp. 993–1030.

Louca, F. and Perlman, M. (2000). *Is Economics an Evolutionary Science?*, Cheltenham, UK: Edward Elgar.

Medlen, C. (2003). "Veblen's Q-Tobin's Q", *Journal of Economic Issues*, 37(4), pp. 967–986.

Minsky, H. (1960). "Financial crisis, financial systems, and the performance of the economy", *Hyman P. Minsky Archive*, Paper 232, available at: http://digitalcommons.bard.edu/hm_archive/232

Minsky, H. (1967). "Suggestions for a cash flow oriented bank examination", *Hyman P. Minsky Archive*, Paper 175, available at: http://digitalcommons.bard.edu/hm_archive/175

Minsky, H. (1970). "Financial instability revised: The economics of disaster", *Hyman P. Minsky Archive*, Paper 80, available at: http://digitalcommons.bard.edu/hm_archive/80

Minsky, H. (1975a). *John Maynard Keynes*, New York: Mc Graw Hill, 2008.

Minsky, H. (1975b). "Suggestions for a cash flow-oriented bank examination", *Hyman P. Minsky Archive*, Paper 17, available at: http://digitalcommons.bard.edu/hm_archive/17

Minsky, H. (1977a). "A theory of systematic fragility", in E.J. Altman and A.W. Sametz (eds.), *Financial Crises: Institutions and Markets in a Fragile Environment*, New York: John Wiley and Sons, pp. 138–152.

Minsky, H. (1977b). "Central Banking and the Behaviour of an Economy", *Hyman P. Minsky Archive*, Paper 81, available at: http://digitalcommons.bard.edu/hm_archive/81

Minsky, H. (1979). "Policy", *Hyman P. Minsky Archive*, Paper 305, available at: http://digitalcommons.bard.edu/hm_archive/305

Minsky, H. (1980a). "Money, financial markets, and the coherence of a market economy", *Journal of Post Keynesian Economics*, 3(1), pp. 21–31.

Minsky, H. (1980b). "Capitalist financial processes and the instability of capitalism", *Journal of Economic Issues*, 14(2), pp. 505–523.

Minsky, H. (1982). *Inflation, Recession and Economic Policy*, Armonk, NY: M.E. Sharpe.

Minsky, H. (1985–1986). "An introduction to post-Keynesian economics", *Economic Forum*, 15(2), pp. 1–13.

Minsky, H. (1986a). "Money and crisis in Schumpeter and Keyens", in H.J. Wagener and J.W. Drukker (eds.), *The Economic Law of Motion of Modern Society: A Marx-Keynes-Schumpeter Centennial*, Cambridge, UK: Cambridge University Press, pp. 112–122.

Minsky, H. (1986b). *Stabilizing an Unstable Economy*, New York: McGraw Hill, 2008.

Minsky, H. (1987a). "Securitization", *Hyman P. Minsky Archive*, Paper 15, available at: http://digitalcommons.bard.edu/hm_archive/15

Minsky, H. (1987b). "The macroeconomic safety net: Does it need to be improved?", *Hyman P. Minsky Archive*, Paper 398, available at: http://digitalcommons.bard.edu/hm_archive/398

Minsky, H. (1990). "Schumpeter: Finance and evolution", in A. Heertje and M. Perlman (eds.), *Evolving Technology and Market Structures: Studies in Schumpeterian Economics*, Ann Arbor: The University of Michigan Press, pp. 51–74.

Minsky, H. (1992a). "Schumpeter and Finance", *Hyman P. Minsky Archive*, Paper 280, available at: http://digitalcommons.bard.edu/hm_archive/280

Minsky, H. (1992b). "Stabilizing and unstable economy: Testing the institutional structure", *Hyman P. Minsky Archive*, Paper 459, available at: http://digitalcommons.bard.edu/hm_archive/459

Minsky, H. (1993). "Finance and stability: The limits of capitalism", Working Paper No. 93, Annandale-on-Hudson, NY: The Levy Economics Institute of Bard College.

Minsky, H. (1995a). "Financial factors in the economics of capitalism", *Journal of Financial Services Research*, 9(3–4), pp. 197–208.

Minsky, H. (1995b). "The balanced budget amendment: A time bomb to subvert American prosperity", *Hyman P. Minsky Archive*, Paper 50, available at: http://digitalcommons.bard.edu/hm_archive/50

Minsky, H. (1996). "Uncertainty and the institutional structure of capitalist economies", *Journal of Economic Issues*, 30(2), pp. 357–368.

Minsky, H. (2013). *Ending Poverty: Jobs, Not Welfare*, Annandale-on-Hudson, NY: The Levy Economics Institute of Bard College.

Minsky, H. and Campbell, C. (1988). "Getting off the back of a tiger: The deposit insurance crisis in the United States", *Hyman P. Minsky Archive*, Paper 67, available at: http://digitalcommons.bard.edu/hm_archive/67

Minsky, H., Papadimitriou, D., Phillips, R. and Wray, L.R. (1993). "Community development banking: A proposal to establish a nationwide system of community development banks", Public Policy Brief No. 3, Annandale-on-Hudson, NY: The Levy Economics Institute of Bard College.

Minsky, H., Delli Gatti, D. and Gallegati, M. (1994). "Financial institutions, economic policy and the dynamic behaviour of the economy", Working Paper No. 126, Annandale-on-Hudson, NY: The Levy Economics Institute of Bard College.

Mitchell, W. (1969). *Types of Economic Theory: From Mercantilism to Institutionalism*, vol. 2, New York: Augustus M. Kelley Publishers.

Mouhammed, A. (1999). "Veblen and Keynes: On the economic theory of the capitalist economy", *Journal of Institutional and Theoretical Economics*, 155(4), pp. 594–609.

Nelson, R. (1995). "Recent evolutionary theorizing about economic change", *Journal of Economic Literature*, 33(1), pp. 49–90.

Nelson, R. and Winter, S. (1982). *An Evolutionary Theory of Economic Change*, Cambridge: Cambridge University Press.

Niggle, C. (2006). "Institutionalist-post Keynesian economics and the post monetarist new consensus", in M. Setterfield (ed.), *Complexity, Endogenous Money and Macroeconomic Theory*, Cheltenham: Edward Elgar, pp. 368–388.

O'Hara, P.-A. (1993). "Veblen's analysis of business, industry and the limits of capital: An interpretation and sympathetic critique", *History of Economics Review*, 20, Summer, pp. 95–119.

O'Hara, P.-A. (2000). *Marx, Veblen, and Contemporary Institutional Political Economy*, Cheltenham, UK: Edward Elgar.

Papadimitriou, D.B. (1998). "(Full) employment policy: Theory and practice", Working Paper No. 258, Annandale-on-Hudson, NY: The Levy Economics Institute of Bard College.

Papadimitriou, D.B. (2008). "Promoting equality through an employment of last resort policy", Working Paper No. 545, Annandale-on-Hudson, NY: The Levy Economics Institute of Bard College.

Papadimitriou, D.B. and Wray, L.R. (1997). "The institutional prerequisites for successful capitalism", *Journal of Economic Issues*, 31(2), pp. 493–500.

Papadimitriou, D.B. and Wray, L.R. (1998). "The economic contributions of Hyman Minsky: Varieties of capitalism and institutional reform", *Review of Political Economy*, 10(2), pp. 199–225.

Papadimitriou, D.B. and Wray, L.R. (eds.) (2010). *The Elgar Companion to Hyman Minsky*, Cheltenham, UK: Edward Elgar.

Peterson, W.C. (1977). "Institutionalism, Keynes and the real world", *Journal of Economic Issues*, 11(2), pp. 201–221.

Peterson, W.C. (1987). "Macroeconomic theory and policy in an institutional perspective", *Journal of Economic Issues*, 21(4), pp. 1587–1620.

Plotkin, S. and Tilman, R. (2011). *The Political Ideas of Thorstein Veblen*, New Haven: Yale University Press.

Raines, P. and Leathers, C. (1992). "Financial innovations and Veblen's theory of financial markets", *Journal of Economic Issues*, 26(2), pp. 433–440.

Raines, P. and Leathers, C. (1993). "Evolving financial institutions in Veblen's business enterprise system", *Journal of the History of Economic Thought*, 15(2), pp. 249–264.

Raines, P. and Leathers, C. (1996). "Veblenian stock markets and the efficient markets hypothesis", *Journal of Post Keynesian Economics*, 19(1), pp. 137–151.

Raines, P. and Leathers, C. (2000). *Economists and the Stock Market*, Cheltenham, UK: Edward Elgar.

Raines, P. and Leathers, C. (2008). *Debt, Innovations, and Deflation*, Cheltenham, UK: Edward Elgar.

Rotheim, R.J. (1981). "Keynes's monetary theory of value (1933)", *Journal of Post Keynesian Economics*, 3(4), pp. 568–585.

Rutherford, M. (1984). "Thorstein Veblen and the process of institutional change", *History of Political Economy*, 16(3), pp. 331–348.

Sardoni, C. and Wray, L.R. (2006). "Monetary policy strategies of the European Central Bank and the Federal Reserve Bank of the United States", *Journal of Post Keynesian Economics*, 28(3), pp. 451–472.

Tavasci, D. and Toporowski, J. (2010). *Minsky, Crisis and Development*, Hampshire, UK: Palgrave Macmillan.

Tcherneva, P. (2011). "Fiscal policy: Why aggregate demand management fails and what to do about it", Working Paper No. 650, Annandale-on-Hudson, NY: The Levy Economics Institute of Bard College.

Tcherneva, P. (2012). "Beyond full employment: The employer of last resort as an institution for change", Working Paper No. 732, Annandale-on-Hudson, NY: The Levy Economics Institute of Bard College.

Tcherneva, P. (2013). "Reorienting fiscal policy: A critical assessment of fiscal fine-tuning", Working Paper No. 772, Annandale-on-Hudson, NY: The Levy Economics Institute of Bard College.

Tcherneva, P. (2018). "The job guarantee: Design, jobs, and implementation", Working Paper No. 902, Annandale-on-Hudson, NY: The Levy Economics Institute of Bard College.

Tilman, R. (1996). *The Intellectual Legacy of Thorstein Veblen*, Westport, Connecticut: Greenwood Press.

Todorova, Z. (2013). "Conspicuous consumption as routine expenditure and its place in the social provisioning process", *American Journal of Economics and Sociology*, 72(5), pp. 1183–1204.

Tugwell, R.G. (1939). "Veblen and Business Enterprise", *New Republic*, 29 March, pp. 215–218.

Tymoigne, E. (2006). "The Minskyan system, Part I: Properties of the Minskyan analysis and how to theorize and model a monetary production economy", Working Paper No. 452, Annandale-on-Hudson, NY: The Levy Economics Institute of Bard College.

Tymoigne, E. (2009). *Central Banking, Asset Prices and Financial Fragility*, Abingdon: Routledge.

Tymoigne, E. (2012). "Measuring Macroprudential Risk through Financial Fragility: A Minskyan Approach", Working Paper No. 716, Annandale-on-Hudson, NY: The Levy Economics Institute of Bard College.

Tymoigne, E. and Wray, L.R. (2014). *The Rise and Fall of Money Manager Capitalism*, Abingdon: Routledge.

Veblen, T. (1898). "Why is economics not an evolutionary science?", *The Quarterly Journal of Economics*, 12(4), pp. 373–397.

Veblen, T. (1899a). "The preconceptions of economic science", *The Quarterly Journal of Economics*, 13(2), pp. 121–150.

Veblen, T. (1899b). "The preconceptions of economic science", *The Quarterly Journal of Economics*, 13(4), pp. 396–426.

Veblen, T. (1899c). *The Theory of the Leisure Class*, Great Clarendon Street, Oxford: Oxford University Press, 2007. With an introduction and notes by Martha Banta.

Veblen, T. (1900). "The preconceptions of economic science", *The Quarterly Journal of Economics*, 14(2), pp. 240–269.

Veblen, T. (1901). "Industrial and pecuniary employments", *Publications of the American Economic Association*, 2(1), pp. 190–235.

Veblen, T. (1904). *The Theory of Business Enterprise*, New York: Charles Scriber's Sons, 1915.

Veblen, T. (1905). "Credit and prices", *The Journal of Political Economy*, 13(3), pp. 460–472.

Veblen, T. (1906). "The place of science in modern civilization", *The American Journal of Sociology*, 11(5), pp. 585–609.

Veblen, T. (1908a). "The evolution of the scientific point of view", *University of California Chronicle*, X(4), pp. 395–416.

Veblen, T. (1908b). "On the nature of capital: Investment, intangible assets, and the pecuniary magnate", *The Quarterly Journal of Economics*, 23(1), pp. 104–136.

Veblen, T. (1909). "The limitations of marginal utility", *Journal of Political Economy*, 17(9), pp. 620–636.

Veblen, T. (1914). *The Instinct of Workmanship and the State of the Industrial Arts*, New York: Macmillan.

Veblen, T. (1919). *The Vested Interests and the Common Man*, New York: B.W. Huebsch.

Veblen, T. (1923). *Absentee Ownership and Business Enterprise in Recent Times: The Case of America*, London: George Allen and Unwin, 1924.

Vining, R. (1939). "Suggestions of Keynes in the writings of Veblen", *The Journal of Political Economy*, 47(5), pp. 692–704.

Whalen, C.J. (ed.) (1996). *Political Economy for the 21st Century*, Armonk: M.E. Sharpe.

Whalen, C.J. (2001). "Integrating Schumpeter and Keynes: Hyman Minsky's theory of capitalist development", *Journal of Economic Issues*, 35(4), pp. 805–823.

Whalen, C.J. (2008). "Post Keynesian institutionalism and the anxious society", in S. Batie and N. Mercuro (eds.), *Alternative Institutional Structures: Evolution and Impact*, New York: Routledge, pp. 273–299.

Whalen, C.J. (ed.) (2011). *Financial Instability and Economic Security after the Great Recession*, Cheltenham, UK: Edward Elgar.

Whalen, C.J. (2017). "Understanding financialization: Standing on the shoulders of Minsky", Working Paper No. 892, Annandale-on-Hudson, NY: The Levy Economics Institute of Bard College.

Wilber, C.K. and Jameson, K.J. (1983). *An Inquiry into the Poverty of Economics*, Notre Dame: University of Notre Dame Press.

Wilson, M.C. (2006). "Budget constraints and business enterprises: A Veblenian analysis", *Journal of Economic Issues*, 40(4), pp. 1029–1044.

Wray, L.R. (1997). "Government as employer of last resort: Full employment without inflation", Working Paper No. 213, Annandale-on-Hudson, NY: The Levy Economics Institute of Bard College.

Wray, L.R. (1998). *Understanding Modern Money: The Key to Full Employment and Price Stability*, Aldershot: Edward Elgar.

Wray, L.R. (2000). "The employer of last resort approach to full employment", Working Paper No. 9, Annandale-on-Hudson, NY: The Levy Economics Institute of Bard College.

Wray, L.R. (2003). "Is Euroland the next Argentina?", Working Paper No. 23, Kansas City, MO: Center for Full Employment and Price Stability.

Wray, L.R. (2007a). "Veblen's theory of business enterprise and Keynes's monetary theory of production", *Journal of Economic Issues*, 41(2), pp. 617–624.

Wray, L.R. (2007b). "Minsky's approach to employment policy and poverty: Employer of last resort and the war on poverty", Working Paper No. 515, Annandale-on-Hudson, NY: The Levy Economics Institute of Bard College.

Wray, L.R. (2016). *Why Minsky Matters*, Princeton, New Jersey: Princeton University Press.

Wray, L.R. (2018). "Functional finance: A comparison of the evolution of the positions of Hyman Minsky and Abba Lerner", Working Paper No. 900, Annandale-on-Hudson, NY: The Levy Economics Institute of Bard College.

Zinke, G.W. (1958). "Veblen's macroinstitutionalism", in D. Dowd (ed.), *Thorstein Veblen: A Critical Reappraisal*, New York: Cornell University Press, pp. 303–317.

Index

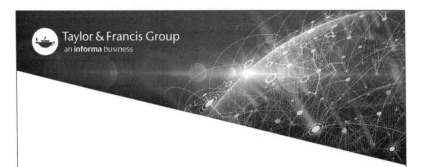

For Product Safety Concerns and Information please contact our EU
representative GPSR@taylorandfrancis.com Taylor & Francis Verlag GmbH,
Kaufingerstraße 24, 80331 München, Germany

Printed and bound by CPI Group (UK) Ltd, Croydon, CR0 4YY
02/05/2025
01859252-0001